Calm

MEDITATION

Made Simple

—

CONTENTS

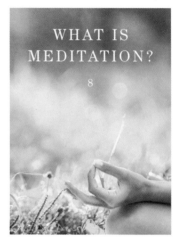

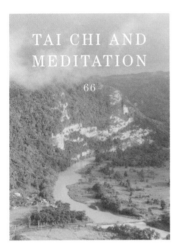
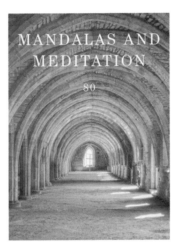
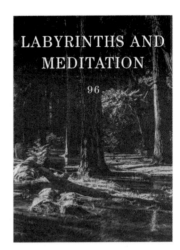
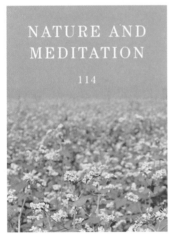

INTRODUCTION

———

When most of us think of meditation, we think of someone sitting cross-legged on a cushion, eyes closed, in deep contemplation. However, there are many different and creative ways to meditate. This book will introduce you to the art of combining meditation with other wonderful health and spiritual practices, such as yoga, Chi Kung and Tai Chi. You will also learn to meditate while colouring mandalas, while walking or tracing labyrinths and while enjoying the beauties of nature.

The first chapter gives you an overall introduction to meditation and offers reasons why you might want to meditate. It includes an explanation of basic sitting meditation, as well as the four types of meditation you will be working with in this book.

The next chapter introduces you to the spiritual origins of yoga and shows you how to enhance your yoga practice by combining specific meditations with various well-known postures, such as Downward-Facing Dog.

The third chapter gives an explanation of the ancient Chinese practice of Chi Kung, and introduces you to the Eight Pieces of Silk Brocade, a powerful set of Chi Kung exercises with meditations to accompany each one.

The fourth chapter explains the origins of Tai Chi Chuan, the world-famous Chinese martial art that has become one of the most popular health

and longevity practices for people, young and old, around the world. You will learn meditations for the first five moves of the Short Yang-Style Form, which will inspire you to create your own personal meditations for the entire set of movements.

The fifth chapter introduces the mysteries of the mandala, an ancient spiritual symbol found in all cultures around the world. You will enjoy combining meditation with colouring four unique mandala drawings that are provided in this book.

In the sixth chapter you will discover the labyrinth as a tool for spiritual growth and healing. Directions are provided for creating your own labyrinth for walking or tracing, and meditations are given for tapping into the labyrinth's power.

Finally, the seventh chapter will encourage you to find time in your busy life to reconnect with nature. You will find a collection of short meditations for practising in various natural environments.

MEDITATION TO ENHANCE OTHER PRACTICES

For all the meditations you may find it useful to record them ahead of time, then play them back so that you can concentrate on the meditation more fully.

What you will discover in this book is that meditation can work in many different settings, and in combination with numerous other practices. For example, bringing meditation to yoga or Tai Chi greatly enhances their effectiveness. By doing so, you bring your mind and body into alignment, creating a synergy that has a powerful cumulative effect over time. You can work on problems, learn to calm your mind and bring a spiritual focus to everything you do. Hopefully, you will be inspired to create your own meditations for different activities that address your specific needs for personal and spiritual development. It is the intention of this book to introduce you to the creative and empowering aspects of meditation, as well as the mysteries and depth of your own beautiful mind.

WHAT IS
MEDITATION?

—

Meditation involves turning inwards to the mind itself. It can be a means of relaxation, a technique for cultivating mental discipline, a way to gain psychological insight or a method of communicating with God or a higher power. The ultimate purpose of meditation is to help you overcome the limitations of ordinary consciousness and expand your mind to higher levels of awareness. This chapter introduces the benefits and basic tenets of meditation, as well as four simple techniques that are used throughout this book.

MEDITATION AS A KEY TO THE MIND

Our everyday lives are like a waking dream. Rather than being truly awake and aware, we are usually preoccupied or lost in thought. One thought triggers another – and another and another. Buddhists affectionately call this ordinary state of mind 'monkey mind', as if our minds were filled with unruly chimps leaping from branch to branch. We may start with one thought and end up with another that is entirely unrelated to the first. Our thoughts seem to have a life of their own.

And it is not just our thoughts that are unruly. A chance meeting or event can trigger our fear, anger, jealousy or desire so instantaneously that we feel hijacked literally by these powerful emotions. One minute we are driving down the road, and the next we are furious because someone has cut us off and almost caused us to have an accident. Or we arrive at work in a great mood, only to have the boss 'push our buttons'. One offhand remark can leave us feeling put out and off balance for the rest of the day.

And if unruly thoughts and emotions are not enough, we also have a habit of projecting onto others what we think they are feeling or thinking, without truly knowing whether this is so; or we ascribe to others qualities that we ourselves desire. For example, we may see a well-dressed handsome stranger at the next table and imagine that he is successful and brilliant, when in truth he is deeply in debt and of ordinary intelligence. Conversely, we may see a casually dressed woman and imagine that she is a dull-witted and lonely, when in fact she is a happily married university professor. Closer to home, we may be afraid that our partner is having an affair when they are not, because unconsciously we may be tempted ourselves. And of course we all have fantasies about the future: about how we would like life to be and what, or who, we would like to have in our lives.

Rather than being awake to reality as it is, and truly aware of what is going on around and inside us, it is as if we are living in a dream world – a small, confining world of our mind's creation. Yet we are convinced that we know what is real and what isn't. The purpose of examining our normal mental state is not so that we can judge ourselves; after all, every person on the planet can relate to these ordinary states of mind. But, as we will discover, the mind is capable of much more, and meditation is a key to its unfolding.

WAKING UP
TO REALITY

When something happens to jolt us out of our usual mental state – such as the loss of a job, the death of a loved one or a diagnosis of serious illness – we feel disoriented and life seems turned on its head. In these moments our usual uncontrolled thinking, our hair-trigger emotions and our projections and fantasies fall away, and we experience reality with a shocking clarity. As painful and intense as these experiences may be, they often cause us to feel truly awake in a way we have never been before.

When tragedy strikes, our priorities change dramatically. What seemed so very important beforehand is no longer significant, and we are led to ask profound questions about the meaning of life. Because of this deep change in perspective, we may eventually consider our hardship a gift, because without it our lives would not have opened and deepened. What is at first a tragedy can sometimes be an opportunity for profound awakening, because our mind is jolted out of our normal 'dream state'.

The good news is that rather than waiting for the world to shock us into awareness, we can choose to live in an awakened state all the time. Meditation is the antidote to living in a dream world. It is the conscious act of training the mind, through a variety of mental and physical techniques, so as to live fully in the present moment. Meditation takes discipline, but it is a rewarding practice that leads to greater concentration, awareness, peace, relaxation and contentment. From this peaceful mind spring insight and awareness. With a disciplined mind we can probe thoughts and ideas more deeply, or create a visualization of how we would like to be. Although it is not necessary to practise a particular religion in order to meditate, meditation can lead to profound spiritual realizations. It has the potential to deepen our understanding of the greater mysteries of life.

THE STORY OF MEDITATION

One of the earliest texts on meditation is the 5,000-year-old Indian Vigyana Bhairava Tantra. It contains 112 meditation techniques for realizing one's true self, written as a series of lovely poems. All 112 meditations are answers, given by the Hindu god Shiva, to questions from the goddess Devi regarding the nature of reality. In this beautiful teaching, instead of answering her questions directly, Shiva gives her methods, or meditation techniques, so that Devi might experience the answers for herself. One of the most famous early meditation masters was Siddhartha, a prince who lived in India 2,500 years ago. He gave up his kingdom, his family, his wealth and a privileged life to pursue spiritual knowledge. After much effort, he became a Buddha or 'Awakened One', and founded the Buddhist religion. It was through meditation that he gained his enlightenment. He taught concentration and mindfulness meditation to help others achieve wisdom, and encouraged meditation on love and compassion for all living beings. He taught that meditation can lead – one person at a time – to bliss, and to the end of human suffering as we know it.

MEDITATION AND RELIGION

The first record of Christian meditation appeared around 220 CE. It was then that the 'desert monks' of Egypt began reading the Bible slowly and carefully, in order to ponder the deeper meaning of each verse. This spiritual practice was called 'divine reading', or Lecto Divina. After 'divine reading', the monks would find themselves in meditation, then in prayer, then in a simple, wordless focus on God, which they called 'contemplation'. Later, this four-part progression – from reading, to meditation, to prayer, to contemplation – became known as the 'ladder' of prayer.

Christian meditation thrived throughout the centuries in numerous forms, and continues to be of great interest to many Catholics and other Christians today. A popular 20th-century meditation is called 'Centring Prayer', and places emphasis on interior quiet and the experience of God's presence.

Most religions teach some kind of meditative practice. For example, a Jewish meditation found within the Kabbalah visualizes a heavenly realm through which the soul navigates in order to achieve spiritual realizations. Within Islam, practitioners perform the Salat, a meditation that focuses on the mind and heart of Allah, five times a day. Contemporary Catholic, Protestant and Jewish faiths have all adapted meditation techniques from Eastern traditions, such as Buddhism.

Meditation has always been used as a tool for achieving spiritual realization, but it is important to stress that religious affiliation is not necessary to practise any form of meditation, even if a particular form originated in a religious context. There are many New Age meditations that derive from Eastern traditions, such as Transcendental Meditation and the school of Natural Stress Relief, which rely on scientific study rather than religion.

FOUR WAYS TO MEDITATE

There are endless meditation techniques, but all boil down to four different ways of working with the mind. In this book we will explore all four kinds of meditation:

- The first involves learning to focus and concentrate – in other words, ways to 'tame the monkey'. By training the mind to focus on an object such as a candle or an image, on the breath itself or even on a movement such as walking, you become aware of your normal uncontrolled thinking patterns and eventually learn to quiet your mind.

- The second involves learning about yourself, and the world around you, without the filters of unbalanced emotion, fantasy or projection. This is sometimes called mindfulness, insight or awareness meditation.

- The third is to contemplate a topic. As already mentioned, the early Christians meditated on passages of the New Testament. Tibetan Buddhists practise 'analytical meditation' on topics such as compassion, patience and generosity.

- The fourth type of meditation engages the mind's ability to imagine or visualize, to help you create the mind and reality you want.

THE
BENEFITS OF
MEDITATION

Throughout its long history, meditation has been associated with spiritual development. Calming the mind was not a goal in itself; rather, meditation provided a base for spiritual enquiry and realization. Meditation was for attaining insight into the meaning of existence and the mind of God. And if you want to deepen your spiritual life, meditation can definitely help you.

Meditation also has many practical benefits, and there is nothing wrong with exploring everything it has to offer –

physical, mental, emotional and/or spiritual. As we shall see, working with meditation in combination with other self-help practices, such as yoga or Tai Chi, or while walking labyrinths or colouring mandalas, will only enhance and expand your experience of this ancient practice. Pages 15–17 offer some of the wonderful reasons to practise meditation.

MEDITATION FOR BETTER HEALTH

Simply meditating on your breath can lower your blood pressure, slow your heart rate and ease your anxiety. And, as an adjunct to traditional or alternative medical treatment, meditation can assist in healing various illnesses, such as cancer and heart disease. It can help you manage pain, and can prevent illness by helping you stay physically balanced and healthy. For example, doctors at an American University in Texas developed a 'Pain and Stress-Management Program' based on a combination of Eastern meditation and yoga. They found that these techniques, when combined with medication, significantly improved patients' pain symptoms, compared to drug therapy alone.

Richard Davidson, a Harvard-trained neuroscientist, and Robert Sapolsky, a Stanford University professor who studied the effects of stress on the body, discovered that meditation can strengthen the immune system, help with depression and lower the levels of cortisol – the hormone associated with stress. Davidson teamed up with meditation teacher Jon Kabat-Zinn and taught meditation to employees of an American biotech firm to help them reduce stress. After eight weeks they found that workers who had received meditation training not only felt less stressed, but had stronger immune systems than the control subjects. Meditation helps to create contentment, peace and joy, which ease your state of mind and, in turn, promote health and longevity.

MEDITATION TO INCREASE CONCENTRATION

Practising concentrated meditation – focusing your mind on one object, such as the breath – helps you develop mental skills that are useful in all areas of your life. Being able to focus will make you more successful in your career, and will make life easier for you and your co-workers. Being able to give your full attention to your partner or child helps them feel respected and loved. On a scientific level, concentration meditation actually causes changes in the brain. Researcher Richard Davidson discovered that during concentration meditation, certain brain waves become synchronized with one another. In other words, meditation positively affects both body and mind.

MEDITATION TO BOOST AWARENESS

Because there is so much stimulation from electronic media, in the areas of work, shopping and entertainment, Attention Deficit Disorder (ADD) is on the rise in the adult population. You may not suffer from clinical ADD, but you may feel overloaded at times and want to 'shut down' as a way to ward off more than you can handle. As a result of multitasking and rushing, you may find that you are losing the ability to be aware of what you are actually doing or experiencing. Try mindfulness meditation if you want to cut through the noise, enliven your senses and enrich your life. Learn to slow down, live in the present and appreciate the life you have. It is interesting to note that at a recent conference for adults with ADD, participants began each morning with mindfulness meditation.

MEDITATION TO BALANCE THE EMOTIONS

Because of how stressful life is today, it's easy to develop a problem with anger. Working long hours, with rising costs, it's no wonder that you feel on edge and get angry at the drop of a hat. World upheaval and unrest can contaminate your life with fear. Competition may cause you to be jealous and resentful of the success of others. If you want to stay conscious of your emotions and monitor your emotional patterns, try meditating. You will find that many of the meditations in this book will help you transform negative emotions into positive ones.

Having mental peace and less emotional reactivity are benefits of long-term meditation practice. Researchers have found that meditating on compassion, for example, can cause positive changes, over time, in a part of the brain known as the amygdala – the area involved in processing emotion.

MEDITATION TO HEAL PSYCHOLOGICAL PROBLEMS

If you have a serious psychological problem, such as chronic depression, be sure to get professional help. If you have an addiction to drugs, food, sex or alcohol, unresolved grief over the loss of a loved one, are facing up to childhood neglect or trauma, or other psychological issues, then meditation is a wonderful way to support yourself during your healing process. It helps you make friends with yourself and let go of self-hate. If you have problems with procrastination, or difficulties maintaining a healthy relationship, meditation can help, too. Let meditation be a great companion on your healing journey. As you will discover, combining meditation with any of the other practices in this book, such as yoga or Chi Kung, is an excellent way to overcome negative habits and patterns.

MEDITATION TO CONTEMPLATE THE MYSTERIES OF LIFE

If you feel bogged down in the materialistic view of the world that pervades our lives, meditate to transform and transcend it. Meditate if you want to understand the meaning of your life, your destiny, your connectedness to all living beings and the sacredness of reality. Spirituality is an overused word, but its root is 'spirit'; it refers to the life force and intelligent energy that pervades the Universe – you may call that God, Buddha, Christ, Spider Woman (an important goddess among south-western Native American peoples) or your higher power. You may or may not have difficulty with organized religion. If you do, simply try to be open to the idea that there is more to life than the material realm. Ask the big questions of life and see what answers you get; create your own spiritual path.

Meditation is a way to care deeply for yourself and others. It affirms to yourself that your life is important, precious and fleeting. No matter what brings you to meditation, or what form you practise, you will definitely find it worth your time.

MEDITATION BASICS

Although they are not essential, there are a few items that you may want to invest in to make your meditation more comfortable and productive. Most can be found online or in specialist shops and book stores that carry meditation supplies. You might also try Buddhist or other meditation centres in your community, since they often sell meditation equipment to their members and to the public.

YOU WILL NEED

CUSHION OR CHAIR

Since it is often recommended that you sit to meditate, you may want to consider buying a cushion made especially for meditation. You will find they come in all shapes, sizes and colours, stuffed with a variety of materials, including kapok and buckwheat shells; some are even adjustable. It's best to try them out first, if you can, and see what feels best to you.

MATS

If you buy a meditation cushion, you may want to invest in a larger, flat mat (often called a zabuton) to go under your cushion. This serves to raise the cushion a little higher off the ground and protect your ankles. For relaxation, and for some meditation poses that require you to lie flat on the ground, you may also want to buy a thin portable yoga mat (available from most yoga schools).

BLANKETS AND SHAWLS

For yoga relaxation poses, you may want to place a light blanket over yourself to keep you warm. Likewise, if you find yourself sitting in meditation for long periods of time, or early in the morning when it might be a little chilly, it's nice to have a blanket or shawl to put around you. Having one of these when you are sitting colouring a mandala or walking a labyrinth helps you stay focused and comfortable.

LOOSE CLOTHING

Try to wear loose clothing when practising sitting meditation or when working with any of the other methods introduced in the next few chapters. Avoid wearing a belt, a watch with a tight wristband or any piece of clothing that is restrictive in any way. Baggy drawstring trousers or sweatpants are great; a long loose skirt or caftan also works well. Some companies make clothing especially for yoga, Tai Chi or meditation, and you can find them online.

CREATING A SACRED SPACE

Sacred space is a place where you can connect with a world beyond your ordinary, everyday one – a site for your meditation and movement practices. It could be a part of your bedroom or living room, or a special place that you create temporarily. If you are lucky enough to have an extra room, make that into your meditation and practice space.

First, decide where you would like your meditation and practice space to be. You may need to rearrange the room you are planning to use. Decide whether your space can be permanent or must be temporary, to be created only when you practise yoga, Tai Chi or meditation. When practising sitting meditation, you will need enough space to accommodate your cushion or chair; when you are doing movement exercises, the area will need to be large enough for you to move around it freely. You may need a small table and chair for work with mandalas or small labyrinths.

Next, thoroughly clean the space you have chosen. Vacuum and dust it, and if you have floors that you can mop, then do so. Wash any slipcovers or cushion covers. Cleaning does not just create a tidy space. It also clears negative energy within you, as well as in your environment. Also, energy can become stagnant, and cleaning enlivens the room.

For sitting meditation, arrange your cushion or chair wherever you would like it to be. Sit down and make sure you feel comfortable in that spot. If you have a yoga mat, a shawl or additional small cushions, store them nearby where you can access them easily. Add a small altar, if you like, with flowers, images of holy figures, candles or incense. If you enjoy listening to music during your meditation or practice sessions, place a CD player nearby.

Remember, your sacred space is utterly personal, and as you meditate and do the other practices outlined in this book, it may evolve over time. When you meditate in nature, mentally create a sacred space around you. By doing this, you honour your intention to live mindfully by providing a special area for your personal and spiritual growth. By creating sacred space, you invite the sacred into your life – observe how this space enriches your life.

BASIC SITTING MEDITATION

As meditation is concerned with taming, healing and awakening your mind – and because your mind and body are inextricably linked – posture is important. When you sit in meditation, or do any of the other practices in this book, you will learn that your body and breath can be a great help to your mind.

When you meditate in nature, mentally create a sacred space around you. You can visualize it as a small circle, closely surrounding where you are sitting, or you can visualize it as expansive and taking in all you can see or imagine. If possible, bring a blanket and sit on the ground. As you settle into your meditation posture, feel the energy of the sky above and the earth below filling your body.

The exercises in this book concentrate on combining meditation with other activities, such as yoga, Tai Chi or Chi Kung. But prior to working with other techniques, it is a good idea to learn basic sitting meditation. The traditional sitting posture for meditation is the one the Buddha taught 2,500 years ago, called the 'seven-point posture'.

THE CLASSICAL SEVEN-POINT POSTURE

Although you may not be able to master the classical seven-point posture right away, it is worth the effort to try and do so. If it seems impossible, do the best you can. If nothing else, keep your spine straight. Correct posture helps your mind find peace, strength and control. It benefits your physical body by bringing your energies and body systems into balance.

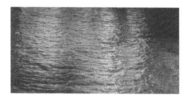

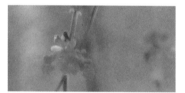

1 Sit on the floor, with your back – from the nape of your neck to the small of your back – as straight as possible. Imagine a pile of coins stacked on top of one another.

2 Cross your legs. Your right leg should be above your left leg. The backs of your feet should sit flat on the tops of your thighs. Ideally, your two feet should make a straight line.

3 Your shoulders should be even and relaxed. Try not to sit with one shoulder higher than the other.

4 Your chin should be level with the floor, and tucked in slightly.

5 Your eyes should be relaxed, open and slightly lowered, looking into space, at nothing in particular, somewhere about 1 m (3 ft) in front of you.

6 Your tongue should be placed against your upper palate.

7 Your lips should be slightly parted, and your teeth should be touching, but not clenched. Breathe through your nose.

HELPFUL TIPS FOR THE SEVEN-POINT POSTURE

- You can use a cushion to raise your bottom a little higher, forcing your knees closer to the floor and helping your back to stay straight. It is best to sit a little forwards on the cushion.

- Your hands should be cradled palms upward, one on top the other, four fingers' width below the navel (not resting on your legs or feet). Your elbows should be held slightly out from your body. If you prefer, simply rest your hands on your knees.

- Although you may want to close your eyes, it is better to train yourself to meditate with open eyes. Closed eyes encourage more thoughts, daydreaming and distraction.

- Try to be as relaxed as possible. Most of us carry a great residual load of tension in our bodies. Unfortunately, the effort to sit in a meditation posture may temporarily produce even more tension. Learn to notice where you're tense or in pain, and release the tension slowly.

- Make adjustments with small micro-movements. The most important part of the posture is keeping your spine straight and shoulders relaxed. If you can't cross your legs in the correct seven-point style, do the best you can, or sit in a chair.

- If you find it is too difficult to sit up straight, because of back pain or injury, by all means use a back support or simply sit in a chair with your feet flat on the ground. Do whatever you can to make the sitting posture work for you.

- If you are coming to meditation later in life, do not torture yourself into thinking that you have to sit in the traditional posture; make any adjustments that you need. One of the goals of meditation is to become a kinder person. So be sure you extend that kindness to yourself.

Although it is wonderful to combine meditation with other activities, sitting meditation should be the bedrock of your practice. If possible, practise sitting meditation on a daily basis. Even if you can only spare ten minutes a day, you will begin to experience many of the benefits already mentioned (see pages 14–17).

CONCENTRATION MEDITATION

Meditating or concentrating on the breath, on a daily basis, provides a solid foundation for all other forms of meditation. Ancient Hindus and Buddhists meditated in this way to tame uncontrolled thinking and reduce negative thoughts and actions, as a way to prepare their minds to be receptive to spiritual truths. Basically, you meditate on your breath in order to give your mind something to 'hang on to' when it starts to jump from one thought to another. Training your mind in this way helps you focus on one thing at a time and develop your powers of concentration. It has a calming influence on your body and mind, and is beneficial for reducing negativity and anxiety, as well as lowering the heart rate and blood pressure.

1 Sit cross-legged on a cushion, with your buttocks slightly raised (if you can't sit cross-legged, sit on a chair). Keep your back straight, your shoulders level and relaxed and your chin parallel to the floor. Lower your eyes and focus about 1 m (3 ft) in front of you. Rest your hands gently on your knees.

2 Breathe normally through your nose, using your abdomen rather than your chest. Check your posture, and relax any part of your body that is tense.

3 Begin counting your breath on each exhalation, and when you reach ten, begin again. Thoughts will intervene and, when they do, simply let them go and return to counting your breath.

4 After ten minutes or so, end the session. Try to bring focus and concentration into your daily life.

MINDFULNESS MEDITATION

When you are awake, your mind jumps from one thought to another, like a monkey leaping from branch to branch. You may have had the experience of driving to the supermarket, getting lost in thought and 'waking up' as you pull into the car park. During the drive you probably had hundreds of thoughts, and countless images and impressions crossing your mind. It was as if the car was on automatic and drove itself to the shop.

This meditation is designed to help you observe your mind and its tendency to jump continuously from one thought to another. It will also help you be more mindful of what you are actually thinking and feeling. Becoming more aware of your emotions and mental patterns will help you become more conscious in your daily life. As a result, you will feel more alive and present in each moment of the day.

1 Sit in your meditation posture on a chair or cushion and take a few deep breaths.

2 Begin to observe your thoughts. Notice how quickly and seamlessly your mind jumps from one idea, impression or thought to another. Think back a few minutes ago and try to remember what you were thinking. Trace how you got to what you are thinking at the moment.

3 Look at a watch or a clock in order to time yourself, and for the next 60 seconds, make hash marks with a pencil on some paper every time your thoughts change during that minute.

4 Bring this new awareness of 'monkey mind' into your daily life. Try to be more mindful of what you are thinking, rather than getting lost in thought.

ANALYTICAL MEDITATION

Anger is one of the most destructive emotions for your health. Meditating on its antidote, patience, will make life more pleasant, both for you and for those around you. In Buddhism, patience means 'forbearance' and refers to that quality of remaining calm in the face of adversity or provocation. Specifically, it means not giving in to your anger. Anger is a strong force within everyone. On a day-to-day level, notice how you can become irritated by the most trivial of things, despite your good nature. The Buddha recommended dealing with anger through meditation, in order to become calmer, more aware of your emotions and more loving of others.

1 Sit on a cushion or chair in your meditation space. Practise watching your breath for five minutes (see page 24) to calm and focus your body and mind.

2 Bring to mind the last time you were angry with someone. Are you still angry? If not, where has your anger gone? Ask yourself if getting angry in that situation helped you or hurt you. Ask yourself if it helped you to become a kinder, more loving person. Think of how you would feel if you were able to give that person more space to be who they are, regardless of how much they irritate you or make you feel angry. Imagine doing that now. Feel the peace that comes over you as you relax and give up the need to fight. Generate a sincere desire for that person to be happy and free of suffering.

3 Come back to the present. Sit watching your breath for another five minutes, then end your meditation.

MEDITATION WITH VISUALIZATION

Television and the Internet provide us with 24-hour, instantaneous news. Often that news is about violence, war and conflict of all kinds. It is easy to feel overwhelmed, hopeless and powerless, or simply to go numb and bury your feelings, only to have them manifest in sleepless nights or other stress-related problems. Practise this meditation when you are feeling afraid, overwhelmed and hopeless about the state of the world.

1 Find a quiet place at home or outdoors. Sit in your meditation posture on a chair or cushion. Breathe deeply for a few minutes.

2 Think about a particular conflict that affects you most. Try not to take sides, favouring one warring group over another. Acknowledge that both the aggressor and those experiencing the aggression are suffering.

3 Generate the desire for all beings involved to heal their anger and pain. Include yourself in this wish. Visualize a sacred being: God, Buddha, Krishna, the Virgin Mary or your higher power. Imagine a cooling and healing white light emanating from that being to you, filling your body and calming any anger or fear you may feel.

4 From your heart, send out light to those at war – to those fighting, to their families and to the leaders who have generated this conflict. Generate a feeling of compassion for yourself and all involved. Visualize the war ending and all beginning to live in peace. End your meditation session when you feel ready.

YOGA AND MEDITATION

—

The original goal of the ancient practice of yoga was spiritual transformation. When you bring meditation to your practice of simple yoga poses, as described on the following pages, this will not only give you a healthier body, but will help you change your mental habits, your attitudes and your outlook on life. It will assist you in expanding your consciousness and will put you in touch with your deeper wisdom.

WHAT IS YOGA?

Today, most of us know yoga as a health practice that has its roots in ancient India. If you attend a yoga class you will learn various *asanas* (postures). The physical benefits of *asana* practice are almost too numerous to mention.

The following is a short list of health improvements that you may experience from ongoing yoga practice:

- The body becomes more flexible.
- Cardiovascular fitness and circulation improve and blood pressure can be normalized.
- Digestion improves through better blood supply to the digestive and eliminative systems.
- Joint function and stiffness improve, extending the range of motion.
- Holding postures enhances muscle tone, strength and endurance.
- Posture improves and back pain is reduced.

- Stress and anxiety are reduced, a sense of calm and well-being increases.
- Spinal health is improved and maintained.
- The endocrine system is balanced and regulated.

Although the physical benefits of *asana* practice are wonderful, you may be surprised to know that in ancient India, yoga was practised as a complete spiritual path to enlightenment. The *asanas* were only one part of that path. They were designed to enhance meditation and encourage spiritual realization. In order to understand the relationship of yoga and meditation, it helps to explore the ancient roots of yoga and its many aspects.

THE EIGHT LIMBS OF YOGA

The most ancient texts on the philosophy of yoga are the Yoga Sutras of Patanjali. Here we learn that there are eight aspects of yoga called 'limbs', which together form the complete path. Below you will find the Eight Limbs of classical yoga. Their names are in Sanskrit, the sacred language of India. The Eight Limbs form a beautiful and inspiring path for physical and spiritual development.

YAMA

Five ethical guidelines regarding moral behaviour towards others:
- *Ahimsa*: Non-violence
- *Satya*: Truthfulness
- *Brahmacharya*: Non-lust
- *Asteya*: Non-stealing
- *Aparigraha*: Non-covetousness

NIYAMA

Five ethical guidelines regarding moral behaviour towards oneself:
- *Saucha*: Cleanliness
- *Santosav*: Contentment
- *Tapas*: Sustained practice
- *Svadhyaya*: Study
- *Isvara Pranidhana*: Surrender to God

ASANA

Yoga postures.

PRANAYAMA

Breathing exercises.

PRATYAHARA

Withdrawing the senses in order to still the mind.

DHARANA

Meditation for focus and concentration.

DHYANA

Meditation for expanding awareness.

SAMADHI

Meditation that brings enlightenment.

THE YOGA PATH TO YOUR INNERMOST SELF

Classical yoga also views human beings as being made up of five *koshas* (layers). The five layers progress from outer to inner: the innermost layer is the Self or *Atman*, known as the eternal centre of consciousness or Absolute Reality. Yoga as a spiritual and meditative practice encourages movement from our outermost layers to our more subtle interior core. A good way to imagine the layers is a series of lampshades of different colours covering our basic pure and brilliant core consciousness, our Self or *Atman*, which is said to have never been born and never to die.

The *Annamaya Kosha* is the physical outer layer composed of our skin, muscle tissue, bones and organs. The opening, strengthening and aligning of the physical structures of the body through *asana* practice is important for physical health, but also opens the *nadis* (energy channels) of the body, enhancing the flow of *prana* (energy), which is important for working with the next layer, *Pranamaya Kosha*. Meditation on awareness of the physical body deepens our overall awareness of life from moment to moment.

Moving inwards, the next layer is *Pranamaya Kosha* (the energy layer), which involves the circulation of our breath and our life energy. *Prana* means 'energy' – it is also known as *Chi* or breath – in other words, that vital force that animates all living beings. Deep and slow breathing while practising *asanas* nourishes your life energy and opens the subtle channels of your body, enlivening your entire being. Meditation focused on awareness of the breath is an excellent choice for working with *Pranamaya Kosha*.

Mana means 'mind', and the *Manamaya Kosha* is the mental layer, the one associated with the nervous system and the one where we process thoughts and emotions. It is at this layer that we address the wandering and overactive aspects of the mind. Meditations that calm the mind and those that help us become aware of thoughts and emotions are important for working with this layer.

REACHING THE INNER LAYERS

Moving towards the centre, *Vijanamaya Kosha* is the layer of wisdom and higher states of consciousness. *Vijana* means 'knowing'. This is the wisdom layer that underlies the thinking aspect of the mind. When we access this layer of the Self, we experience a deeper knowing, a communion with the Divine (however we envision it) and insight into our essential nature. This inner layer is the one that yearns for Truth and drives us to search for deeper meaning in our lives. Meditations that focus on *Vijanamaya* concentrate on the expansion of consciousness, beyond thinking and our ordinary reality.

The last and innermost layer before the Self is *Anandamaya Kosha*, also known as the body of bliss. It is the innermost subtle layer of the Self. It is at this level that we experience freedom, peace and union with the Divine. This is not bliss as an emotional high; rather, it is joy and love beyond what thought can comprehend, and unrelated to any reason or cause. You simply rest in bliss.

At our centre, the realization of the Self or *Atman*, using the metaphor of the lamp and lampshades, is the light itself. It is the indescribable experience of

enlightenment, the goal of yoga meditation. However, do note that meditation that brings you to the *Anandamaya Kosha* and the realization of *Atman* is not the focus of this book. These levels are only achieved with long-term practice and with the help and guidance of an authentic teacher.

The Eight Limbs of yoga and the five *koshas* demonstrate that, for the ancients, yoga was meditation. Hopefully, this will inspire you to begin combining meditation with your own yoga practice.

SIMPLE POSTURES AND MEDITATIONS

Try the following simple poses or *asanas* paired with introductory meditations designed to help you stabilize your mind, increase your awareness and expand your consciousness.

MOUNTAIN POSE

The Mountain Pose, or *Tadasana*, is the start and finish point of all standing yoga poses. It is called Mountain Pose because ideally your mind is quiet and your body is strong and still, like a mountain. When practising this pose at home, try combining it with meditation on the breath, to simultaneously increase your awareness of your thoughts and feelings and help calm your mind.

1 Stand with your feet together and your arms relaxed at your sides.

2 Rock forwards and backwards gently until you find a place where your feet feel grounded and balanced. Feel the weight of your body evenly on all parts of your feet – heels, toes, inner and outer edges – and press down to make as full contact with the floor as possible.

3 Keep your knees straight and your kneecaps relaxed. Make sure your knees are directly over your ankles and your hips directly over your knees. The muscles in your legs should be engaged, but not tensed.

4 Let your breath quieten to its own rhythm. Relax your shoulders and let your arms hang naturally, with your wrists and hands heavy at your sides.

5 Draw your pubic bone in so that your buttocks protrude, then bring your bottom back into alignment by tucking the tailbone in slightly.

6 Breathe in through your nose, lift your chest up away from your belly and feel your spine extend upwards through the crown of your head. Then draw your chin in slightly, but keeping it parallel to the floor, enabling the back of your neck to lengthen. Relax your throat.

7 As you breathe out, press down again firmly through your feet and feel the opposite pull of energy upwards through your spine.

MOUNTAIN POSE MEDITATION

1 As you stand in Mountain Pose, breathe deeply for a few moments to relax your body and clear your mind of any worries or fears. Then let your breath settle into a natural rhythm.

2 Begin by counting your breath, focusing on the out-breath. Count up to ten and then begin all over again. As you pay attention to your breath, notice any thoughts that arise. As soon as you notice them, return to focusing on your breath. You may do this endlessly, but don't worry, just keep returning to your breath. Do this with gentleness and kindness towards yourself, without judgement, as if you were taking a small child by the hand and leading him or her back to your side. Do this as long as you are comfortable.

3 Continue counting your breath, but this time notice any feelings that may arise: perhaps frustration, agitation or boredom, or anger about a past encounter with someone you dislike. Do not judge yourself for having these feelings, and do not 'fan the flames' by entertaining them, but instead notice them, accept them and return to focusing on your breath.

4 When you are ready to end your meditation, take a series of deep breaths and slowly release your Mountain Pose.

SEATED FORWARD BEND

Seated Forward Bend, or *Paschimottanasana*, is a simple pose that, combined with meditation, can help you get in touch with the vast expanse of your inner being. On a physical level, it helps stretch your spine, shoulders and hamstrings, and stimulates your kidneys and liver. Mentally, it can help you relieve stress and depression. On a spiritual level, it offers a great opportunity for you to explore your inner landscape and experience the potential of meditation to open you to higher states of consciousness.

1 Sit on the floor with your buttocks supported on a folded blanket and extend your legs straight out in front of you. Tilt your pelvis back to tip your weight onto the front of your sitting bones. Press your hands into the floor beside your hips and lift your torso towards the ceiling.

2 Inhale as you lift your arms above your head, keeping your front torso long. Exhale and lean forwards from the hip joints, not the waist. Lengthen your tailbone away from the back of your pelvis. If you can, grab the sides of your feet with your hands. If you can't reach that far, loop a strap around the soles of your feet. Make sure your elbows are straight and not bent.

3 After a few breaths, try to go further. Do not use your hands and arms to pull yourself into the forward bend; instead, lengthen your torso into the pose, keeping your head and neck in line with your vertebral column.

4 With each inhalation, lift and lengthen your front torso slightly, and with each exhalation extend a little more. In this way your torso will lengthen imperceptibly with the breath.

SEATED FORWARD
BEND MEDITATION

1 After you settle into *Paschimottanasana*, close your eyes and reflect on the fact that you are much more than your physical body. Consider that you have a vast inner landscape, where your dreams, memories and intuition come from. Know that this inner realm is the most important aspect of who you are as a person. It is where you connect with your higher self, your higher power, God – whatever or whomever you want to call it.

2 Begin to focus on your breath, relax and with each inhalation feel this vast expanse grow within you. Feel your interior transparent self expand to fill your city, then breathe in again and expand it to fill your country. Breathe in again and expand it into the entire vast Universe itself.

3 Generate a feeling of love and compassion for the entire Universe – especially for yourself. Rest in that feeling of expansive love and caring.

4 When you are ready, open your eyes and begin to gather your consciousness back from the Universe to your country, then to your city, then to yourself as you are in *Paschimottanasana*.

5 Begin to release your pose on an inhalation, draw in your upper abdominal area towards your spine, then raise your arms and chest upwards, returning to your starting seated position.

6 How has this meditation changed your sense of yourself?

CHILD POSE

Child Pose, or *Balasana*, is a resting pose practised between other *asanas*. Because it is a tonic for the spine, it not only clears your mind, but rejuvenates and energizes your entire being. More importantly, it requires you to surrender your body to gravity and embrace the art of 'doing nothing'. On a spiritual level, it encourages a sense of appreciation, devotion and gratitude, and the ability to offer your gifts to others without expecting anything in return.

1 Kneel on the floor and sit back with your feet together and your buttocks resting on your heels. (If you have difficulty doing this, place a folded towel or blanket between your thighs and calves.) Separate your knees by about the width of your hips. Place your hands on your thighs, palms down.

2 Inhale deeply, then exhale as you fold yourself forwards, place your chest to rest between your thighs and rest your forehead on the floor. Bring your arms around to your sides until your hands are resting on either side of your feet, relaxed, with the palms up and fingers slightly curled. Release any tension in your shoulders and let them fall towards the floor, naturally opening the space between your shoulder blades.

3 Breathe gently through your nose and feel your breath expanding into the back of your torso, as it lengthens and widens your spine. Let go and relax completely.

CHILD POSE MEDITATION

1 As you come to rest in Child Pose, inhale naturally through your nose, relaxing and surrendering into the moment with each breath. With your head touching the earth, offer yourself as you are to the Universe. Generate a feeling of complete acceptance and compassion for yourself and all other beings.

2 Notice that your spine is curved the way you were in the womb. Enjoy the safe, secure feeling of the Child Pose. Take a moment and imagine what it was like to be in your mother's womb. Express appreciation to your mother for the gift of life.

3 Now, as you breathe through your nose, visualize your breath moving towards the back of your spine and filling the space between each of your vertebra. Appreciate the centrality of your spine to your life, health and well-being. As you breathe into your back, feel each breath calming your nerves and increasing the circulation around your spine.

4 Visualize the nerves from every one of your organs – your heart, lungs, liver, kidneys – connecting to and running through your spinal cord. Feel this improved circulation having a positive impact on every one of your bodily functions, including your blood pressure, digestion and thought processes. If you have any health problems or illness, use your breath to bring healing energy first to your spine, and then through it to the part of your body that needs healing.

5 As you release from Child Pose, feel a renewed gratitude and appreciation for your life, your spine and its importance to your health and well-being.

CORPSE POSE

Corpse Pose, or *Savasana*, is the ultimate resting pose. When practised with guided meditation, it can bring feeling to parts of your body that may be cut off to your awareness. Being fully aware of your body and accepting it as it is, helps you increase your love and compassion for yourself and others.

1 Lie down on the floor with your legs stretched out and your feet slightly wider than your hips. Place your arms at about 45 degrees to your body with your palms facing upwards and your hands and fingers relaxed.

2 Tuck your chin in slightly and allow your shoulders to soften and melt into the floor.

CORPSE POSE MEDITATION

1 First, flex your right ankle, then tense your foot, your calf muscle and your knee and slightly contract your thigh muscle. Now tighten your whole right leg. Hold, then breathe out and release, letting all the tension flow out through your foot. Feel your entire leg. If any emotions arise, such as anger or sadness, accept them.

2 Repeat this procedure with your left leg. Keep breathing deeply and slowly through your nose, breathing out any remaining tension. Whether they are fat, thin, young or arthritic, love and accept your legs as they are.

3 Now squeeze your buttocks one at a time and then together as tightly as you can. Release and feel the tension flowing away. Let yourself fully feel your pelvic area and any emotions that may arise. Love and accept your sexuality as it is.

4 Focus on your lower and upper abdominal muscles, draw your navel back towards your spine as far as you can, then breathe out and release, allowing all the tension to drop away. Love and accept your stomach area as it is now.

5 Bring your awareness to your back muscles. Tense those muscles. As you breathe out, let your muscles sink down into the floor. Feel compassion for yourself and the difficulties you bear at this moment in your life.

6 Contract your chest muscles as tightly as you can, then release, breathing out any tension. Let go of any grief that you may carrying.

7 Next, bring your awareness to your shoulders. Tighten your right shoulder muscle. Then release it, letting the shoulder sink into the floor. Do the same with your left shoulder. Appreciate how well you bear the weight of your responsibilities.

8 Tense your right arm muscles, and squeeze your hand and fingers as tightly as you can, lifting your arm slightly off the floor. Then release, and feel the tension flowing down and out of your fingertips. Do the same with your left arm. Accept and love your arms as they are.

9 Focus on your neck and head. Tense the muscles of your neck and throat. Clench your jaw tightly and scrunch up your whole face, then release it. Love and accept your beautiful face.

10 Continue to lie in deep relaxation, generating a feeling of self-acceptance for as long as you like.

TREE POSE

Tree Pose, or *Vrksasana*, helps develop mental concentration, which allows you to calm your mind. It enhances physical and emotional stability, improves balance, strengthens the legs and increases hip flexibility. The challenge of the Tree Pose is maintaining your balance on one leg. If you have trouble balancing, it is often the result of having a restless mind or distracted attention. Regular practice of this posture will help you learn to focus and concentrate.

1 Begin by standing in Mountain Pose (see pages 34–35). Breathe naturally for a few breaths.

2 On an in-breath, shift your weight onto your left foot. Exhale and bend your right knee, grab your right foot and place the sole as high as possible onto your left inner thigh, with the toes pointing straight down. Find your balance, then gently draw your leg back to open your hip.

3 Bring your palms together in the prayer position at your heart level, keeping your eyes focused on a point in front of you to assist your balance.

4 Inhale and raise your arms just above your crown, keeping your palms together and stretching upwards through your fingertips.

TREE POSE
MEDITATION

1 Visualize the foot you are balanced on as the root of the tree and your leg as the trunk. Imagine that your right leg, head and arms are the branches and leaves. You may be unsteady and find your body moving back and forth, but try not to break your concentration. Find a point straight ahead and focus on it.

2 Try to empty your mind of extraneous thoughts and actually feel that you are a huge, solid, rooted oak tree standing silently in the woods. You may move very slightly with the wind, or even a lot in a storm, but you always stand firm, tall and grounded. Keep your eyes steady and focused on an object in front of you in the forest. Breathe naturally.

3 Imagine birds landing on your 'branches' and squirrels climbing up your 'trunk'. They are comfortable with you because you are steady, strong and calm. You generously welcome their presence, yet they do not distract you or cause you to lose your focus and concentration. You are calm and centred in yourself.

4 The moment your thoughts go somewhere else – to work, your fears, anywhere else at all, and they will – you may fall off balance. Readjust your posture and gently bring your focus back to your visualization of a beautiful, strong, balanced, calm, majestic tree. Feel in your body that you are that tree.

5 Rather than berate yourself for losing balance, try congratulating yourself for holding the pose as long as you did. Use this opportunity to become aware of how very powerful your thoughts are and how unbalancing they can be in your daily life.

6 Return to Mountain Pose and rest. Now try this meditation in Tree Pose balancing on your other leg.

DOWNWARD-FACING DOG

Down Dog, as this is called for short, or *Adho Mukha Svanasana*, is one of the poses in the traditional Sun Salutation sequence, and is an excellent yoga *asana* practised on its own. This pose is so named because it resembles a dog stretching itself. On a physical level, it is strengthening and invigorating. On a spiritual level, it helps with not creating tension, either in your *asanas* or in your life.

When there is an absence of tension, you have an opportunity to let go of any preconceived ideas and meet life on its own terms. For example, if you hear some bad news, instead of physically and mentally tensing up, you can drop into your breathing and let the feelings move through your body. In the same way, instead of coming to quick judgements in a situation that provokes anger, releasing tension and focusing for a moment on your breath gives you space to deal with the situation as it is. Life is taxing enough without adding tension. Because Downward-Facing Dog is a challenging pose, the tendency is to add more muscle tension than is necessary to maintain it. It provides a great opportunity to work with the idea of not adding tension.

1 Start on your hands and knees. Place your knees directly below your hips, and your hands under and slightly forwards of your shoulders. Turn your toes under.

2 Exhale while lifting your knees up from the floor, then lift the sitting bones of your buttocks towards the ceiling. Make sure your middle fingers point forwards, and press your palms evenly into the floor.

3 Then with an exhalation, push your thighs back and stretch your heels down towards the floor. If your heels come fully to the floor, step your feet back to give yourself more of a challenge. Straighten your knees, but be sure not to lock them.

4 Feel your shoulder blades, then widen them and draw them towards your tailbone. Keep your head between your upper arms, but do not let your head hang.

5 If you have difficulty aligning your head between your shoulders, try raising your hands off the floor on a pair of yoga blocks, or use the seat of a metal folding chair.

DOWNWARD-FACING DOG MEDITATION

1 Scan your body and find any places where you have introduced more tension than you need. Release any unnecessary tension and relax further into the pose.

2 Think of a recent event where you felt stress. Notice whether this thought causes you to tense your muscles. Now again release the tension, while continuing to remember the stressful event.

3 Empty your mind of any thoughts and concentrate on your breath for a count of ten. Feel the contrast between thinking of a stressful event and tensing your body, and releasing the tension and dropping into your breath.

4 End the meditation by resting in Child Pose (see pages 38–39) for as long as you desire.

LION POSE

Yoga has used nature and wildlife as inspiration for many *asanas*. Lion Pose, or *Simhasana* ('the powerful one'), is an excellent pose for tapping into your personal power. It is an unusual *asana* in that it benefits your face, eyes, jaw, mouth, throat and tongue. It helps with problems like teeth grinding and chronic tension in the jaw. It's even been called an anti-ageing *asana*, as it helps to firm the neck and chin.

On a spiritual level, *Simhasana* helps you access the fierceness of the lion in order to clear negative habitual patterns. In this case, fierceness and wrathfulness are not the same as aggression. Rather, they are a manifestation of your own wisdom or higher power that cuts through your negativity. When you feel demoralized by addictions to food, drugs or alcohol, this is a great pose to inspire confidence that you can indeed overcome them.

1 Kneel on the floor and cross the front of your right ankle over the back of the left. Drop your tailbone towards the floor and straighten your spine.

2 Press your palms firmly against your knees. Fan the palms and splay your fingers like the claws of a lion.

3 Close your eyes and inhale deeply through your nose. Lean forwards a little, then simultaneously open your mouth wide and stretch your tongue out, curling its tip down towards your chin. Open your eyes wide, roll them back and gaze up to your 'third eye'. Contract the muscles on the front of your throat, and exhale the breath slowly out through your mouth with a distinct 'ha' sound. Your breath should pass over the back of the throat to create a 'roar'.

4 Draw your tongue back into your mouth and close your eyes. Sit in meditation before beginning another round (from step 3).

5 Roar three times. Then change the cross of your legs and repeat the procedure the same number of times.

LION POSE
MEDITATION

  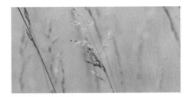

1 After completing steps 1 and 2, sit quietly for a moment and bring to mind any problems you are having with addictions. They can be as simple as being addicted to television, the Internet or ice cream, or more serious problems with drugs or alcohol. Admit to yourself that you have a problem and generate the sincere intention to overcome it.

2 Now close your eyes and imagine that you are your higher power in the form of a lion. Feel strength in your body and clarity in your mind. Know that when you access your wisdom, you access your hidden stores of strength and power, with which you can overcome your addictions.

3 Think of the addiction you want to clear from your life and 'roar' to bring your energy and strength to bear on the problem. If you have been feeling weak and hopeless in the face of your addictions, now experience your strength and resolve.

CHI KUNG AND MEDITATION

—

In parks all across China, millions of people practise Chi Kung exercises on a daily basis for a healthy mind, body and spirit. Chi Kung is the art of circulating, nourishing and cultivating *Chi* or energy, considered one of the 'Three Treasures' of the human being; the other two are *Jing* or essence, and *Shen* or spirit. Chi Kung works directly with *Chi*, but affects all three Treasures. Combining the following Chi Kung exercises with focused meditation and visualization enhances their effectiveness in balancing body, mind and spirit.

WHAT IS CHI KUNG?

Chi Kung (pronounced 'Chee-GUNG') is an aspect of Chinese medicine that combines movement, meditation and regulation of breathing to enhance the flow of *Chi*. In ancient Chinese texts, *Chi* is seen as the vital element that generates and unifies the Universe. It is the energy that pervades all reality. *Chi* is produced by the interaction of Yin and Yang, the two opposite forces of the Universe. It is often translated as 'energy', 'vital energy', 'breath' or 'vital breath'. The word *Kung* means 'work' or 'technique'. Chi Kung, then, means 'energy cultivation'.

In Chinese belief, Heaven and Earth are the parents of all beings. Humans and all other sentient beings live between Heaven and Earth, and are understood to be their offspring. We are alive thanks to our inner *Chi*, our original vital energy that we got from our parents and will lose at death. While we are alive, our *Chi* is nourished by breathing, eating and by physical and mental activity. Besides getting nourishment from breathing and eating, we can regulate our *Chi* through appropriate physical exercise and meditation. *Chi* circulates in our bodies like the blood and lymph. If we do not maintain good circulation of our *Chi*, blocks and stagnation can develop. If our *Chi* does not circulate properly, we do not function at our best and may even develop serious illness or chronic diseases.

HOW IT WORKS WITH MEDITATION

Chi Kung is a health practice with strong meditative and metaphysical aspects designed to help us nourish and enhance the *Chi* we received from our parents, and tap into the fundamental *Chi* energy of the Universe. Chi Kung directly works with *Chi* energy for the purpose of integrating body, mind and spirit. Some Chi Kung exercises help you increase your store of *Chi*; others assist you in moving and circulating it by using your mind and meditative techniques. By working with *Chi* energy, Chi Kung can help you prevent and heal illness; you can also develop a spiritual relationship with nature and the Universe. With advanced practice you can learn to transfer your *Chi* to others and help them replenish their depleted energy.

Chi Kung also recognizes and makes use of the meridian system of Chinese medicine – the pathway of *Chi* – and combines it with the meditative power of focused intention. Its gentle movements slowly build strength and vitality and enhance the immune system. By combining physical and breathing exercises with visualization and focused intent, Chi Kung becomes a powerful practice for mental, physical and spiritual development.

THE THREE TREASURES

In the Taoist tradition there are three 'Treasures' that are considered essential to life. These are known as *Jing*, *Chi* and *Shen*, usually translated as 'essence', 'energy' and 'spirit'. *Chi* is the most well known in the West, but the ultimate goal of all Chinese healing arts is to nourish, balance and enhance all three Treasures.

Jing, or essence, is your genetic inheritance. It is the energy stored in your body that helps you handle stress on a daily basis. It is associated with the hormones of the reproductive and other glandular systems. Your mental sharpness and general physical strength are also controlled by *Jing*. The Chinese say that *Jing* is stored in your kidneys.

When your *Jing* is strong, you remain youthful. When it is weak, you may suffer physical and mental decline or a shortened lifespan. Your *Jing* is naturally used up by living, but it can also be damaged by chronic stress and overwork, emotional imbalance, drug or alcohol abuse, chronic illness and excessive sexual activity.

Chi, the second Treasure, is the source of vitality and energy. Through the constant play of the dual forces in life – Yin and Yang – change occurs, which enables life to exist. *Chi* is the result of the activity of Yin and Yang. The nature of *Chi* is to move, nourish and protect. Chi Kung focuses on the cultivation of *Chi* energy.

Shen, the third Treasure, is the spirit that directs and informs your *Chi*. *Shen* reflects the highest aspect of yourself, and is expressed as love, compassion, generosity, patience, enthusiasm and wisdom.

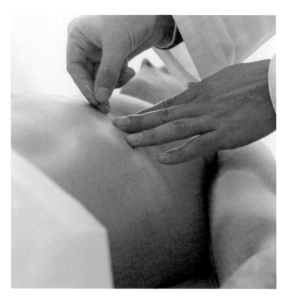

CHI KUNG THROUGH THE AGES

References to *Chi* are found as far back as 1800 BCE. The oldest references to Chi Kung are found in Taoist books from the Tang Dynasty (618–905) that describe breathing, visualization or meditation techniques, aimed at helping one reach immortality. These exercises, practised to enhance health and balance body and mind, were developed, refined and passed down over the centuries from teacher to disciple as closely guarded secrets. Today Chi Kung practices are no longer shrouded in secrecy and are widely available to anyone who wants to learn, both in China and in other parts of the world.

Over the centuries, Chi Kung became strongly associated with the practice of Chinese medicine, and today millions of people in China and around the world regularly practise it as a health-maintenance exercise. Chi Kung exercises are often 'prescribed' by traditional Chinese doctors along with acupuncture and herbs as treatment for various illnesses. In 1989 Chinese hospitals officially recognized Chi Kung as a medical technique and included it in the Chinese National Health Plan. In China it is now possible to get an advanced university degree in Chi Kung.

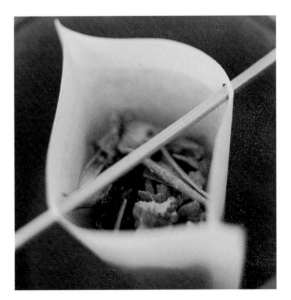

CHI KUNG
IN MARTIAL
ARTS

Chi Kung is also an integral part of the practice of Chinese martial arts. In what are called the 'internal martial arts', the practitioner learns to cultivate and control his or her *Chi*, making it possible to project it outwards and use it as a force against an opponent. You may have seen extraordinary demonstrations on television, such as martial artists breaking bricks with their foreheads, bending iron bars with their bare hands or 'throwing' a person 6 m (20 ft) by emitting *Chi* energy directed at them. These showy *Chi* practices, besides being enormously entertaining, provide insight into the power of working with *Chi* energy. Both the Chinese martial arts of Tai Chi and Kung Fu include the practice of Chi Kung.

CHI KUNG AS A SPIRITUAL PRACTICE

As Chi Kung practices became more standardized, the spiritual or meditative aspects grew in importance. Chi Kung was practised in Taoist, Buddhist and Confucian monasteries for health and spiritual development, and as *Chi* training for the martial arts. The mixing of Chi Kung with Chinese medicine, spirituality and martial arts is best exemplified in the famous Shaolin Monastery in China, the historical setting you may recognize in many contemporary Chinese martial-arts films.

The story is told that a famous Buddhist teacher, Bodhidharma (448–527 CE), created a set of 18 exercises for the Buddhist monks at the Shaolin Temple. These became known as the '18 Hands of the Lohan' or 'the art of the breath of the enlightened ones'. They are exercises for cultivating the Three Treasures of *Jing*, *Chi* and *Shen*.

In ancient times the monks at Shaolin Temple practised meditation, Chi Kung and martial arts. They learned to cultivate their *Chi* through Chi Kung exercises, and their mind and spirit through meditation. The practical health benefits of Chi Kung kept the monks free of illness and enabled them to recover easily from martial-arts injuries. The spiritual benefits of Chi Kung included the unblocking of *Chi* energy, which led to higher states of consciousness. For Chinese spiritual masters, the cultivation of both body and mind were essential to enlightenment.

THE EIGHT PIECES OF SILK BROCADE

The Eight Pieces of Silk Brocade are at least a thousand years old, yet they remain immensely popular in China today. Millions practise them on a daily basis. Combine these movements with meditation and you will have a powerful routine for healing body, mind and spirit.

THE BASIC CHI KUNG POSTURE

All of the 'Eight Brocade' exercises begin with the following basic Chi Kung posture. Simply standing in this posture, while emptying your mind of all thoughts, can be beneficial.

1 Stand with your feet shoulder-width apart and either parallel or slightly turned outwards. Let your hands hang loosely at your sides and relax your shoulders. Allow your fingers to curve and remain slightly apart.

2 Imagine that your whole body is suspended from a string at the top of your head. Unlock your knees and bend them very slightly. Your eyes should be looking forwards, and your chin dropped slightly to release any tension in your neck.

3 Relax your hips and stomach; neither your stomach nor buttocks should be sticking out.

4 Breathe naturally by inhaling and exhaling through your nose keeping your mouth closed.

BA DUAN JIN, OR THE EIGHT PIECES OF SILK BROCADE

The Eight Pieces of Silk Brocade (*Ba Duan Jin*) is an elegant set of eight Chi Kung exercises first described in an ancient 8th-century Chinese text. In this Taoist treatise the 'Eight Brocades' were attributed to one of the eight immortals of Chinese folklore and were developed to guarantee a long life. They work by strengthening and encouraging the free flow of *Chi*, toning the organ systems and clearing the mind of any delusions or negativity. Some experts say that the first eight of the Shaolin Temple's '18 Hands of the Lohan' exercises are the same as those in the Eight Pieces of Silk Brocade.

ONE: REACHING FOR THE SKY

1 Stand in the basic Chi Kung posture (see opposite page), with your feet shoulder-width apart, your shoulders relaxed and your arms hanging loosely at your sides. Close your eyes, calm you mind and breathe regularly. Open your eyes and look forward. Interlace your fingers, with the palms facing down, then slowly raise your arms in a circle above your head, so that your palms face up towards the sky. Inhale as you stretch upwards and at the same time rise up on your toes.

2 As you exhale, come back down, with your feet resting flat on the floor. Keeping your arms in the same position, drop your hands slightly towards your head. Rest for a moment, inhale and stretch upwards again, rising on your toes, but this time with your palms facing downwards. (Side view)

Repeat eight times, alternating the direction of your palms each time.

SUPPORT THE SKY WITH BOTH HANDS MEDITATION

• As you practise this movement, meditate on what the Chinese call the 'Triple Burner': the areas between the collarbone and the diaphragm, the diaphragm and the navel, and the navel and the groin. The Upper Burner is made up of the heart and lungs; the Middle Burner of the spleen and stomach; and the Lower Burner of the liver, intestines, bladder and kidneys.

• As you breathe in, imagine golden light entering your body through your nose and clearing any problems you may be having with your breathing, digestion or elimination.

• As you breathe out, visualize any illness or imbalance exiting your body as grey smoke. Do three repetitions of the First Brocade for each Burner.

TWO: SHOOTING THE GOLDEN EAGLE

1 Begin in the basic Chi Kung posture (see page 56). Step out to the right, bend your knees and take a 'horse-riding' stance. Make sure that you keep your back straight and your buttocks tucked under.

2 Gently raise your arms so that your hands face your chest as if you were holding a beach ball.

3 Look to the left. Inhale and extend your left arm out to your left, parallel to the floor, with your palm and fingers pointing upwards at a right angle. Simultaneously raise your right elbow to your right, parallel to the floor, as if drawing the string of a bow. You should now look like an archer, body facing forwards and head turned to the left. Pull the 'string' back and stretch your left arm leading with the flat of your hand. Breathe out as you stretch.

4 While breathing in, slowly bring your hands back round to the 'beach ball' position (see step 2).

Repeat the exercise to the right. Repeat three times on each side.

DRAW THE BOW TO EACH SIDE MEDITATION

- This exercise emphasizes the kidney area and the waist muscles. In order to generate *Chi* effectively, imagine that you are actually holding a bow and pulling back the string. As you aim your bow, visualize your kidneys being bathed in warming sunlight.

- The emotion ruled by the kidneys when they are imbalanced is fear. Bring to mind anything you are afraid of.

- Visualize your fear dissolving into a mist as the sunlight warms and rejuvenates your lower back area.

THREE: TOUCHING HEAVEN AND EARTH

1 Stand with your feet parallel and shoulder-width apart. Raise your hands in front of you, as if you were holding a beach ball.

2 With your eyes facing forwards, breathe in and raise your left hand above your left shoulder, palm upwards and parallel to the floor, as if carrying a tray. Your right hand should be palm down parallel to the floor. Breathe out as you straighten both arms, pressing the left hand towards the sky and the right hand down to the floor. Keep your palms flat and at right angles to your arms.

3 Relax and breathe in as you bring your arms back to the 'beach ball' position in front of you (see step 1).

Repeat the exercise reversing the position of your hands. Repeat three times on each side.

MEDITATION

- This exercise works on your stomach, spleen, liver and gall bladder. As you alternate raising one hand and lowering the other, you stimulate *Chi* circulation in your stomach area.

- Visualize the organs strengthening and rejuvenating. Imagine any stagnation or toxicity being cleared out as you breathe in golden light. Breathe out any illness or disease as grey smoke.

- The stomach and spleen in disharmony manifest worry and anxiety. If you have a habit of worrying or suffer from chronic anxiety, visualize letting go of whatever you are worrying about at this moment.

- Let a sense of peace and calm wash over your body and mind.

FOUR: COW TURNS TO LOOK AT THE MOON

1 Begin by standing in the basic Chi Kung posture (see page 56). Extend and circle your arms in front of you as if holding an imaginary beach ball or large balloon.

2 Breathe out as you turn your entire upper body from the waist to the left. As you turn, face your palms outwards, as if pushing the beach ball away from you. Keep your feet flat on the floor so as to be able to draw energy from the earth as you do this exercise. Turn back to your starting position and rest for a few moments.

Do the same movement, but turning to your right. Repeat three times on each side.

MEDITATION

• This exercise is said to reduce the effects of negative emotions such as anger, hate and excessive desire, which can damage Yin organs such as your heart, lungs and liver. If you feel angry, excessive *Chi* will accumulate in your head area. This exercise will help redistribute your *Chi* and assist it to flow evenly.

• As you practise this exercise you can meditate on your breath to calm your emotions.

• Visualize any negative emotions leaving your body on the out-breath. Breathe in cooling, soothing white light in their place.

• When you turn to look to the rear, visualize any negative emotions being discarded and left behind you.

FIVE: WILLOW COOLS ITS LEAVES IN THE STREAM

1 From the basic Chi Kung stance (see page 56), raise your right hand and arm over your head, with the palm facing downwards. Raise your left heel. As you breathe out, bend over your left side. Let your left arm and hand hang down naturally at your side, with your palm facing out.

2 Put your weight into your right leg and let your left heel lift off the ground. This will increase the outward arc on the right side of your body. Try to hold this position while remaining as relaxed as possible. Now increase your stretch, bending as far to the left as possible.

Breathe in as you return to the basic Chi Kung posture (see page 56). Now do the same stretch to the right side. Stretch four times to each side. As you stretch, remember to keep your head, neck and spine in alignment.

MEDITATION

- This exercise helps with excessive *Chi* or fire in the area of the solar plexis. Heartburn is one manifestation of excess fire.

- When *Chi* becomes excessive in the heart area, the Chinese turn to the lungs to put out the fire. In Chinese five-element theory, all organs are assigned an element. The lungs are considered the metal element and as such they absorb the heat of the heart or fire element.

- As you stimulate your lungs by compressing them on one side and stretching them on the other, you pull the fire away from your heart area and regulate your *Chi*.

- As you do this exercise, visualize any excessive *Chi* in your heart region smoothing out and normalizing. You can also meditate on the benefits of having a calm body and mind.

SIX: WHITE CRANE WASHES ITS WINGS

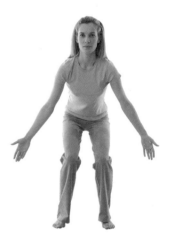

1 Start in the basic Chi Kung posture (see page 56). Pull your arms backwards, then raise them out to the sides at shoulder height. Then bring them forwards, with the palms facing down. Begin to bend your knees slightly.

2 Now lower yourself into a squatting position and bring your hands low enough to brush the tops of your feet.

3 Slowly straighten while rotating your wrists and moving your arms back and around to shoulder height.

Repeat eight times.

MEDITATION

- This exercise has to do with strengthening the kidneys. When you bend over, you restrict the flow of *Chi* to your kidneys. When you stand up again, the *Chi* rushes back. This constricting and releasing removes any stagnation in your kidneys. When your kidneys are strong, your life energy is strong.

- As you do this exercise, meditate on ageing, impermanence and the need to care for your body and mind. Becoming aware of impermanence will help you make better choices in the time you have left.

- Keeping your body strong and healthy through Chi Kung exercises will promote longevity.

ALTERNATIVE POSTURE

1 Alternatively, you can simply bring your hands from the side to the front, then exhale as you bend over, sliding your hands down your legs, and touch your toes.

2 Move your hands to the back of your ankles and inhale as you come up, letting your hands move along the backs of your legs.

3 Let them rest on your buttocks as you resume the straight stance and rise up on your toes. Hold your breath, then exhale and rest with your feet flat.

Rising up on your toes will help improve your balance and strengthen the muscles in your ankles and feet. By flexing your calf muscles, you stretch the bladder meridian that runs along both sides of your spine and down each leg.

Repeat eight times.

MEDITATION

• As you practise this version of the exercise, meditate on how you might maintain better emotional balance on a daily basis, and how fear may be holding you back in your career and relationships.

SEVEN: PUNCH WITH AN INTENSE GAZE

1 Start in the basic Chi Kung posture (see page 56), with your knees slightly bent. Fix your eyes wide open in an intense gaze to help raise your energy. Breathe as you fold your thumbs into your fists and pull them back, palms upwards, at your waist.

2 Breathe out and slowly extend your left arm into a punch. As you extend your left fist, rotate it so that it ends up palm down. At the same time pull your right elbow and fist back. Hold the position for a beat, then alternately extend your right and left arms into punches, drawing the opposite elbow back and rotating your fists as you do so, ensuring the foremost fist is facing palm down and the back fist is facing palm up. (Side view)

Repeat eight times on each side.

MEDITATION

- This exercise clears out any stagnant *Chi*, especially in the liver. The eyes are related to the liver, and opening your eyes in an intense stare helps to raise your energy and access the liver *Chi*.

- When you do this exercise, you draw up *Chi* from the earth, circulate it through your entire body and extend it out from your fists and eyes.

- Even though you are punching, this exercise is not about muscular strength. Rather, it is designed to strengthen the flow of your internal *Chi*, as well as assist the flow of blood and oxygen.

- As you do this exercise, visualize your *Chi* coming up from the earth and flowing through your body and out your eyes and hands.

- Meditate on the importance of keeping *Chi* flowing freely through your body.

EIGHT: SHAKING THE TAIL FEATHERS

1 Start in the basic Chi Kung posture (see page 56), with your knees slightly bent. Breathe deeply for a few moments to clear your mind. Place the backs of your hands on either side of your lower back. (Front view)

2 Begin bouncing up and down from your knees, keeping your feet flat on the floor. Keep your shoulders and elbows loose and relaxed. If you feel tension anywhere, bounce into it until it releases. As you bounce, your hands will give your lower back a massage. Breathe out in short bursts as you bounce. When you inhale, breathe in smoothly. (Side view)

Bounce until you have completed nine exhalations and inhalations.

MEDITATION

- This bouncing exercise will loosen your energy and invigorate your entire body.

- As you bounce up and down, empty your mind of all thoughts and concentrate on the feeling of *Chi* moving through your body. Don't label it as weak or strong, or good or bad; and don't judge yourself if you don't feel what you think you should feel.

- Try not to think. When thoughts enter, simply return to focusing on your body and the *Chi* energy coursing through your organ systems, brain, muscles and bones.

- Visualize the *Chi* coming up from the ground and down from the heavens. Imagine it filling your body and flowing through it.

- When you have finished bouncing, rest in the basic Chi Kung posture (see page 56).

TAI CHI AND MEDITATION

—

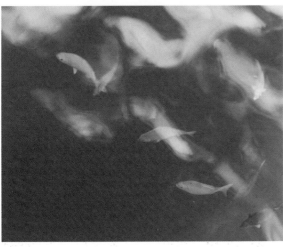

Tai Chi is perhaps the most well-known Chinese physical art and is practised in almost all countries around the world. What began as a martial art has now become a treasured health practice that nourishes body, mind and spirit. The slow, graceful movements – some of which are described here, in combination with appropriate meditations – are lovely to watch and even more enjoyable to perform. Young and old can benefit from this ancient practice.

WHAT IS TAI CHI?

The term *Tai Chi Chuan* can be translated as 'Supreme Ultimate Force'. The notion of 'Supreme Ultimate' refers to the Chinese concept of Yin and Yang, the idea of a dynamic duality that pervades all things. Yin and Yang manifest in the duality of male and female, active and passive, dark and light, forceful and yielding, and sun and moon. The symbol of Tai Chi is the dark/light circular Yin/Yang symbol. The 'Force' refers to the martial aspect of *Tai Chi Chuan*.

The practice of *Tai Chi Chuan* (or Tai Chi) consists of learning a sequence of movements called a 'form'. Many of these movements were originally derived from the martial arts and are actually kicks, punches, strikes and blocks. However, in Tai Chi these movements are performed in graceful slow motion, with smooth, seamless transitions.

For most Tai Chi enthusiasts, the focus is not on martial arts, but on health and longevity. All ages can practise Tai Chi, and most people find it a great stress reliever. But it also can be a wonderful practice for chronic conditions such as arthritis or high blood pressure. As in Chi Kung,

one of the purposes of Tai Chi is to encourage the circulation of *Chi* within the body, thereby enhancing health and vitality. Practising the form also helps with balance, spinal alignment and motor control, and Tai Chi is especially helpful for the elderly in preventing falls. It can help foster rhythm and grace in everyday movement and improve posture. Areas of the body that were chronically tense can be released. Tai Chi is sometimes called 'moving meditation' because learning and practising the form builds focus and concentration. Over time, Tai Chi can help calm the body and mind, and can open the practitioner to deeper spiritual realizations.

TAI CHI'S TAOIST ROOTS

Although Tai Chi was developed as a martial art, its roots lie in the Chinese philosophy of Taoism, a mystical Chinese tradition associated with the scholar Lao Tsu, who lived in the 6th century BCE. He is perhaps best known as the author of the classic Chinese text, the *Tao Te Ching*. Lao Tsu promoted a calm, reflective, mystical and individualistic view of the world that relied heavily on the beauty and tranquillity of nature. In China today, Tai Chi is almost exclusively practised outside in nature, and is still associated with the calm, serene, yielding philosophy of Taoism.

The physical origins of Tai Chi Chuan begin in the 3rd century CE with a physician named Hua-t'uo, who taught a health practice called the 'Movement of the Five Animals', which consisted of imitating the movements of the tiger, deer, bear, ape and bird. He believed that the body needed exercise to help with digestion and circulation, and that only by exercising could one live a long and healthy life. His teaching was probably the precursor of Tai Chi.

As already mentioned, in the 6th century CE the Buddhist teacher Bodhidharma came to the Shaolin Monastery and, seeing that the monks there were in poor physical condition from too much meditation and insufficient movement, created the '18 Hands of the Lohan' Chi Kung exercises (see page 55), which became incorporated into Kung Fu and Tai Chi movements. The movement of *Chi* energy through the practice of these exercises opened the energy channels of the body and facilitated meditative realizations. Later, in the 8th century CE, other Kung Fu movements were created, such as Play the Guitar and Single Whip, which survive today in contemporary Tai Chi forms.

A DREAM OF TAI CHI CHUAN

Taoist monk Chang San-feng, who lived in the 14th century, is considered to be the father of *Tai Chi Chuan*. After much observation, Chang concluded that most martial forms were too vigorous and relied too heavily upon physical strength. One day he witnessed a combat between a snake and a bird. The noise of this confrontation had disturbed his meditation, and so he emerged from his monk's cell to watch. He observed the bird diving down and pecking and clawing fiercely at the snake, although the snake, through its supple movements, was able not only to avoid the attacks, but to initiate strikes of its own. However, when the snake attacked, the bird simply circled and used its wings to deflect the strike.

Chang had a dream that night in which the emperor visited him and instructed him to teach the secrets of the Tao that the bird and snake had demonstrated. The next day he set about creating a new meditative martial art that relied upon internal *Chi* power and the Taoist principles that yielding overcomes aggression and that softness overpowers hardness.

By linking some of the older animal exercises and Shaolin Kung Fu movements with the Taoist notion of Yin and Yang, and his ideas about softness versus aggression, Chang created the fundamental '13 Postures' of Tai Chi. These postures corresponded to the eight basic trigrams of the I Ching (or Book of Changes), an ancient Chinese system of divination, and to the five elements of Chinese medicine – water, wood, metal, fire and earth. His new martial art of Tai Chi Chuan relied on slow, meditative movements, and on focus and concentration on the internal *Chi* energy of the body.

Today, there are many schools of Tai Chi in China and around the world, and the forms have grown from 13 to hundreds of different movements. Yang, Wu and Chen styles are the most well known – all named after the families who created them. Of these, the Yang style is the most popular. The Short Yang-Style Form is the easiest Tai Chi form to learn and the most accessible to people of all ages and physical abilities.

THE SHORT YANG-STYLE FORM

This Tai Chi form was created in the 1950s. It is the national Tai Chi form for mainland China and the world's most popular version of Tai Chi. It contains many of the main movements from the original 108-movement Yang-Style Long Form, but leaves out the numerous repetitions. Because the sequence can be completed in five to eight minutes, it is well suited for people with busy lives who want the health and spiritual benefits of Tai Chi.

MEDITATIONS ON THE SHORT YANG-STYLE FORM

The following meditations are based on the first five movements of the Short Yang-Style Form. If you feel inspired, you can create your own personal meditations for the remaining movements of the form. Each movement flows into the next in one continuous flowing motion.

ONE: OPENING

1 Stand facing south, with your feet together (point your toes out slightly if more comfortable). Relax your shoulders and tuck in the base of your spine. Your spine should be aligned properly; it helps to imagine that it is suspended by a 'golden thread' from above.

2 Sink your weight into your right foot and raise your left foot, placing it down to the east, about shoulder-width from your right foot. Adjust your right foot so that both are parallel and facing south. Your weight is now evenly distributed on both feet. Make a space under your arms, as if you have a large egg under each armpit and turn your hands so they are palms down, fingers pointing forwards.

3 As you breathe in, and while keeping your arms, wrists and fingers relaxed, let your arms float upwards to about chest height. Your forearms should be parallel to the ground and your shoulders relaxed and still.

4 As you breathe out, slowly raise and straighten your fingers so that the tips are facing south. As you do this, your wrists should stay relaxed and drop slightly.

5 Breathing in, make a small movement to draw your elbows back while keeping your arms slightly away from your sides. Draw them back only as far as is comfortable, trying not to create any tension in your back and shoulder blades.

6 Now breathe out, lower your arms slowly to your sides and let your weight sink. Relax your shoulders, hands and fingers and allow your knees to bend slightly. Imagine roots going down into the ground from your feet, and the golden thread attached to the top of your head going up into the sky.

MEDITATION

- The opening move of the Yang form is a moment full of possibilities, like every other part of our lives. Yet unless we can empty our minds of their constant thinking and strategizing and be fully present in the moment, we miss the many opportunities that we have for growth and change.

- As you begin, take a moment to focus on your breath. Scan your body and notice how you feel. Notice any areas of tension. Do not judge yourself if you feel tension in many places in your body – perhaps in your neck, your shoulders or your arms. Simply observe the tension and breathe into wherever the tension is held.

- Continue to focus on your breathing, and feel your breath as *Chi* circulating throughout your body. There is a place on the bottom and centre of your foot just below the ball called Yung Chuan or 'Bubbling Well', where Yin earth energy enters the body. As you breathe, visualize *Chi* being drawn up from the earth though Yung Chuan. As you lift your arms in the form, imagine that they are being lifted by your internal *Chi* energy, rather than by your muscles.

- As you drop your arms and rest in the opening position, meditate on your breath for as long as you like. Feel the nourishing Yin energy create a sense of relaxation and stillness, yet an openness and readiness for whatever life brings.

TWO: TURN RIGHT

1 Inhale as you sink your weight onto your left leg, raise the toes on your right foot and turn slowly to the west by pivoting on your right heel. As you turn, raise your right arm, with the wrist loose and palm down, and draw in your left arm, with the wrist loose and palm up, as if you are holding a large ball of *Chi* in front of you.

2 Exhale as you place your right foot flat on the ground and shift your weight onto your right leg. Your knee should appear to be slightly extended over the tip of your toes as you look down. Your right hand should be at about chin height, and your eyes should be looking beyond it, as if gazing at a distant horizon. Try to feel the ball of *Chi* between your palms, as this feeling of energy between your palms continues throughout the form. Eventually you will not need to visualize the ball of *Chi*, but will simply feel the *Chi* naturally. As you move, keep your back straight and your shoulders relaxed.

Feeling the ball of *Chi* between your palms is the beginning stage of learning to feel *Chi* energy as it moves throughout your entire body. You can also use your mind to move *Chi* by visualizing where you want it to move. Moving *Chi* with your mind is useful for dissolving painful energy blockages and for energizing areas that seem to be lacking in feeling.

When you first learn this movement, you may feel you need to work on the hand and foot movements separately. Like driving a car with manual transmission, eventually the movement of your hands and feet will coordinate without you having to think about it.

MEDITATION

- This second move brings you into confrontation with the future. What awaits you on the horizon? Some ancient sages have said that if you want to know your future, just look at your life at this moment. If you continue living your life as you have been, where will you end up? Do you want to end up in a different place? If so, what will you have to change now in order to create the future you want?

- Sometimes it is not necessary to actively change through force of will. You can also work to dissolve blockages in your body and emotions that have been holding you back from having the life you want. When you release energy blockages in your body, as well as long-held pent-up emotions and negative thought patterns, you increase the free flow of *Chi*. And when your *Chi* flows freely, it helps you to access deeper levels of consciousness. Your mind and heart can then begin to work together to create the life you most desire.

- As you move into this second posture of the form, actively feel the *Chi* energy held between your palms. Scan your body for any energy blockages, and mentally move the *Chi* to that area until you feel the blockage release. Feel the Yin *Chi* flow up from the Earth and the Yang *Chi* flow down from the Heavens and fill your body, dissolving the emotional and physical blockages that are holding you back.

- After you meditate in this way, return your gaze to the horizon. Be open to, and accepting of, change and transformation, and a future full of creative possibilities and spiritual realizations.

THREE: WARD OFF LEFT

1 Breathing in, sink onto your right leg and raise your left heel, as you prepare to step to the south with your left foot. Raise your right hand slightly and face it to the south.

2 Breathing out, step out with your left foot and bend your left knee as your weight moves forwards. As you step out, your left forearm should rise to a horizontal position in front of your chest, with the palm facing inwards. Simultaneously drop your right arm to your side, with the palm facing to the back. Pivot a little on your right heel to release any tension in your right knee. As you move your arms, your palms should feel as if they are stroking each other at a distance as one rises and the other falls. At the completion of the move, your head, hips and shoulders should be in alignment and again facing south, as you were at the start.

MEDITATION

- In this move you meet with the first wide stance of the form. This stance establishes a solid foundation for your posture. As your weight sinks into the centre of your *Tan Tien*, or lower abdomen, and is rooted down into the earth through your feet, you will feel grounded and balanced. If you are balanced and grounded in this move, and someone tries to push you from any direction, you will be able to resist their force.

- In life, this is a metaphor for being rooted and grounded in your own authenticity. If you are spiritually rooted and emotionally grounded, you do not let life push you around. You consider the opinions of others, but do not allow them undue influence over your mind and psyche. You are capable of 'warding off' negative thoughts and any other assaults from people or your environment. You have strong personal boundaries, and your grounded, authentic nature makes it easy for you to have loving, respectful relationships with others.

- As you practise this move, visualize – and feel – that you have all the qualities mentioned above. Know that you have the strength and courage to ward off any negativity or manipulation from others, while maintaining your sense of loving kindness towards all.

- Don't worry if you struggle with these aspects of your life. Meditating on them while practising Ward Off Left will strengthen your ability to be your authentic self.

FOUR: GRASPING
THE BIRD'S TAIL

1 Inhale as you shift your weight onto your left leg and raise your right heel. Turn slightly to your left and again hold an imaginary ball, with your left hand on top and your right hand, palm up, supporting it from below.

2 Exhale as you turn and step to the west with your right heel, into a wide stance. Bend your right knee and bring your weight forward (about 70 per cent) onto your right leg. Pivot on your left heel until any pressure is off your left knee. Your right knee should be over your right toe. The 'ball' you hold now becomes smaller. Your right hand should rise to chest level, slanting upwards and a little to the right. Your left hand should now be much closer to the right, facing downwards and pointing to the palm of your right hand. Your head, hips and shoulders should be squared and facing west.

MEDITATION

- The poetic name of this move, Grasping the Bird's Tail, deserves a closer look. The Chinese characters that make up its name, *Lan Que Wei*, give us clues to its meaning. The first, Lan, means grasping or taking something into your hands in order to examine it. The second, *Que*, means a bird or something small. The third, *Wei*, means the tail, feathers of a bird's body. In the context of Tai Chi, the name of this move suggests the need to pay attention to, and be aware of, the smallest details of the form. It can also suggest the need to be aware of the minor details of life. For example, the seemingly insignificant aspects of a situation, or a person, may hold the key to unlocking its meaning or mysteries. If you are a detective trying to solve a crime, it is the single hair on the coat that may end up convicting the criminal. When you are trying to get to know someone, a small gesture may hold the key to understanding that person's character. And when performing your job, it is often attention to detail that makes the difference between mediocrity and excellence.

- As you practise Grasping the Bird's Tail, imagine that you are gently grasping a tiny sparrow in your hand in order to examine its tail feathers closely. Visualize bringing that attention to detail into a situation at work. Then bring your attention back to the form itself. Make sure that your feet, hands and body are comfortable and correctly positioned.

FIVE: ROLLBACK AND PRESS

1 Inhale and begin by shifting most of your weight onto your left leg. Roll your hands slightly so that your left palm is now facing up, as well as your right palm. The angle of your right elbow should now be more acute, so that your right forearm is more or less pointing upwards and your left palm is cupping your right elbow. Rotate your waist slightly to the right.

2 Finish your in-breath and, without moving your feet, turn your waist towards the left. Draw your left hand and arm back and around, while you lower your right arm until it is horizontal. Keep a feeling of connection between your hands, even though they are now distant from one another.

3 Exhale and bring your weight forwards again onto your right leg by rotating your waist clockwise. Now both of your hands should meet. Your right palm is facing in and your left palm is touching the right and facing out. Your hips and shoulders are facing west and your right knee is over the toes of your right foot.

MEDITATION

- This move is about meeting force with a sideways move, diverting the energy to one side. The greater the force of the attacker, the more off balance he or she will be. This is followed by pressing forwards and following the opponent's energy, then adhering to it in close contact. You are not harming him or her, but you are not being a doormat, either.

- When you are in conflict with someone, it is better to move with their energy than to clash head-on. As you move aside, their own energy propels them into the void. You maintain your integrity and can press forwards from a balanced place. Staying in contact means that you are still in a relationship with them and have a chance to resolve your differences.

- As you practise Rollback and Press, think of how you can learn to flow better with the punches of life and maintain your balance. When should you confront, and when should you just step aside and let judgements and hurtful statements pass you by? Do you have to win at all costs, or can you turn aside and let someone else be 'right'? How can you stay with a relationship when things get rough? How can you use your energy in a responsible and creative way to resolve arguments and differences?

- As you practise this move, imagine that you are in a difficult business meeting, or in an argument with your partner. How can you negotiate this conflict without harming yourself or the other person? Simultaneously, feel in your body the connection with the other person, your own strength and your ability to yield.

MANDALAS AND MEDITATION

———

The mandala is a sacred circle. It is an image or a structure that symbolizes the mysteries of the cosmos, the Universe of a deity, a spiritual journey or the circular nature of time. The mandala is also an ancient tool for expanding consciousness. Meditating on a mandala – and colouring one of the four examples shown in this chapter, as a meditative process – is a practice that can bring you into deeper knowledge of yourself and the sacred nature of all reality.

WHAT ARE MANDALAS?

The word *mandala* means 'circle' in the ancient Indian Sanskrit language, and the mandala is a circular symbol representing psychological and spiritual wholeness. It suggests the circular organization of life itself. The mandala represents the entire cosmos, from the smallest cell to the largest planet.

Mandalas have been drawn, painted or constructed in all cultures, from ancient to modern, to symbolize a spiritual reality. Perhaps this is because the circle is the fundamental form of all creation. Consider the round-shaped cells in our bodies and in any living thing. Think of the stars and the planets – all round forms moving in circular patterns. Consider ancient architecture such as the Pantheon in Rome, a circular building with a name meaning 'to honour all gods'. And consider the beautiful circular labyrinth on the floor of Chartres Cathedral, there to draw visitors into themselves and the experience of this place of worship and contemplation.

The circle is timeless and universal, and the mandala is an ancient circular form used to symbolize sacred truths. Mandalas have a powerful primordial energy and, because of that energy, are wonderful tools for meditation and spiritual development.

MANDALAS AS A HEALING TOOL

In modern times, the psychologist Carl Jung painted small mandalas on a daily basis as a way to access his own unconscious mind, as a tool for his own psychological and spiritual development and as an aid for integrating all aspects of his personality. In his work, the mandala became the container for the good, the bad and the unowned aspects of his self, which he referred to as the 'shadow'. He discovered that by acknowledging and integrating all parts of his psyche he could achieve 'individuation', the joy of feeling complete and whole as a human being. His creation and painting of mandalas became a meditation on his own psychological and spiritual evolution.

Drawing and painting your own mandalas is a wonderful healing practice. You can simply use a dinner plate to make a circle and then add colour, line, shapes and images with pen and paint, or you can make a collage of images that attract you. As you work, observe what emerges and then contemplate its meaning for your life. Another useful practice is to meditate while colouring pre-drawn mandalas based on ancient examples from different cultures.

WESTERN MANDALAS

In medieval Europe, Christians created beautiful mandalas, or rose windows, in their cathedrals as a vehicle for teaching the uneducated masses about the mysteries of the Church. At the centre of the window there is often an image of Christ or Mary. Surrounding the main figure you will frequently find symbols of the seasons of the year, the zodiac, the elements, the virtues and the vices, or perhaps images of the saints and the apostles. If you visit Notre-Dame in Paris, in the north window you will see depicted the kings and prophets of the Old Testament. In the south window of the cathedral at Beauvais you will see the story of Genesis and the Temptation in the Garden. The west window of Chartres Cathedral tells the story of the Last Judgement.

These round rose windows were not only meant to teach, but were intended for use as vehicles for meditation and contemplation. Simply looking at these magnificent jewel-like windows, with their dazzling display of colour and light, can induce a meditative state. Tracing their sacred geometry with your eyes will open you to the deeper messages and symbols contained within the panes of glass. The circular mandala functions to draw you into the middle, often to the image of Christ himself; it forms the sacred Universe of the Divine presence at the centre.

EASTERN MANDALAS

In Buddhist and Hindu cultures, yogis use mandalas as an aid to meditation. For them, the centre of the mandala represents the infinite, or the ineffable godhead, and the source of all creation. By meditating on the mandala, they deepen their understanding of the ultimate meaning of reality, and experience the merging of the self with the Divine.

Of all cultures around the world, Tibetan Buddhists make the most extensive use of mandalas for meditation. Their mandalas are, in essence, two-dimensional paintings of a three-dimensional Universe. They can represent Buddhist deities dwelling at the centre of their sacred environment, or they can depict the entire Universe itself as sacred. Every intricate detail of each mandala has been passed down over the centuries and has specific symbolic meanings.

Because Tibetans have a nomadic culture, they often paint their mandalas on portable, rolled-up canvases known as thankas. They also paint them as frescoes on monastery walls. Perhaps the most fascinating Tibetan mandala is the sand mandala. On special occasions, monks spend weeks creating a very intricate mandala drawing made of coloured sand, depicting a deity at the centre of his or her sacred environment. After the sand mandala is complete, it is used for meditation. Then it is swept up and disposed of in a river or lake, in order to spread the teachings and blessings of the mandala. The practice itself is a wonderful teaching on reducing attachment to material things and accepting that all things are impermanent.

Tibetans also create three-dimensional mandalas for use as 'mandala offerings'. In this practice, a symbolic offering of the entire Universe is made to the guru or teacher. The small ritual-offering set is made of gold or silver and, during the offering rite, is filled with grain and semi-precious or precious stones. For Tibetan Buddhists, the drawing, construction and contemplation of various kinds of mandalas helps to purify bad karma and create positive merit. Meditation on the deity who dwells within the mandala, or sacred Universe, brings the practitioner closer to enlightenment. Through extensive meditation, eventually the practitioner regards everyone as a deity, and all environments as sacred. Ordinary reality is transformed into an enlightened Universe.

COLOURING MANDALAS AS MEDITATION

Colouring mandalas can be profoundly healing for body, mind and spirit, as it leads to a deep sense of relaxation, calm and well-being. Art therapists use mandala colouring to help children deal with illness or process emotional or physical trauma. Smokers who are trying to quit often colour mandalas, because it keeps their hands occupied and relieves the stress of withdrawal. When you combine the healing qualities of colouring mandalas with the conscious act of meditation, they can become a powerful tool for spiritual development.

Here are a few tips for working with mandalas in this way:

- For the best results, copy and enlarge the mandala onto a separate piece of paper. This will make it easier to colour, and will enable you to repeat the meditation as many times as you desire.

- Before you begin, gather a variety of coloured pencils, pens, crayons, chalks, markers and paints that you may want to use. You will not know what feels right until the meditation has begun. Whatever medium you use, make sure that you have a variety of colours across the spectrum, from warm to cool.

- Practise colouring mandalas when you can be alone and undisturbed. If possible, colour them while in your sacred space (see page 20). Light a candle before you begin to signify to yourself that this is a sacred activity.

- Stay focused on the process and meditate as you colour. Keep this book beside you and open to the relevant meditation, so that you can refer to it as you go.

COLOUR AND THE CHAKRA SYSTEM

Chakras are energy centres in the body that run along your spine, from the base of the spine to the crown. Relating the colours that you use to the chakra system will help you associate your meditation with the healing energies of colour:

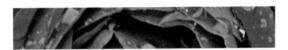

RED

This is associated with the root chakra at the base of your spine and is linked to survival and the physical plane.

ORANGE

This colour is linked to the sacral chakra at your groin and relates to your emotions and sexuality.

YELLOW

This is the colour of the solar plexus chakra and has to do with personal power and autonomy.

GREEN

This is the colour of the heart chakra, which governs love and compassion, as well as integration of mind/body and male/female energies.

BLUE

This is associated with the throat chakra and has to do with communication and creativity and your ability to speak the truth.

INDIGO

This is linked to the space between your eyebrows, which is called your third eye chakra. It governs creative thought and wisdom.

VIOLET

This colour is associated with the crown chakra and connects with Divine, spiritual energy.

When you have completed colouring your mandala, notice the colours that you used and what they might mean for you in the context of that particular meditation.

MANDALA MEDITATIONS

The following meditations provide mandalas in outline form for you to colour as you meditate on self-acceptance, finding your true self, and the vastness of space and time.

MEDITATION ON SELF-ACCEPTANCE

1 Close your eyes and breathe normally for a few minutes. Try to make a mental separation between your everyday world and this meditation session. Bring the positive and negative aspects of yourself into consciousness. Are you controlling? Are you fearful? Are you an extraordinary teacher? Perhaps you are a wonderful parent or a gifted athlete.

2 Open your eyes and mentally place your positive and negative aspects on various parts of the mandala. Are you proud of your positive qualities, embarrassed about your negative aspects? Begin colouring the mandala and, as you do so, try to generate a feeling of complete acceptance for each aspect of your being.

3 When you finish, note where you placed different aspects of yourself on the mandala and what colours you used. Was a negative aspect in the centre or off to the side? Are the colours harmonious or jarring? How does it feel to look at the completed mandala?

4 Finally, note the emergence of any unknown aspects of yourself. Now review your negative aspects and find their hidden positive qualities. For example, you may be overbearing and pushy: think of a time when being pushy was necessary to get a job done or to make your way though bureaucracy. If you are addicted to alcohol and can't find anything positive about it, know that if you heal yourself you could be invaluable to others with the same problem. Meditate on your completed mandala and generate unqualified acceptance and compassion for yourself and all others.

MEDITATION ON FINDING YOUR TRUE SELF

1 Sit in the meditation posture for five minutes (see page 21). Think for a minute of the different personas you present to different people. Do you behave inconsistently in front of your boss, your friends, your spouse, strangers? Become a few of these many personas in your mind by imagining that you are having conversations with different people in your life. What aspect of yourself are you putting forward with each one? Do not judge yourself, or feel that you are being false. We all present different aspects of our personality in different situations.

2 Now try to imagine your essential self, your best self, the one who is without artifice or neurosis. Imagine that you are free of any negativities or delusions, and that you are filled with love and compassion for all beings. Imagine that you possess complete wisdom and knowledge. Imagine that you are enlightened.

4 When you reach the centre, imagine that you have reached your more authentic, loving, compassionate self. Meditate on your true self for as long as you desire.

3 Begin colouring the mandala on the facing page. As you colour, work from the outside in and feel yourself moving through your various personas, negativities and delusions to the centre – your essential core self. Your true self is the enlightened being that resides within. Buddhists would call this your inherent Buddha-nature.

5 Hang up your mandala where you can see it every day to remind yourself of who you really are.

MEDITATION ON THE VASTNESS OF SPACE

1 Sit in meditation for a few minutes to calm your mind. Close your eyes and think of the stars and planets and of the vast, inconceivable space that makes up the cosmos. Imagine that you are looking at Earth from a point in space, and then focus on where you live on our tiny fragile planet. Now imagine that you are still in space, but you turn away from Earth and look out into the vast unknown. Note how it feels to be floating in space. Where is up? Where is down?

2 Mentally return to Earth, open your eyes and begin colouring the centre of the mandala, working outwards. As you colour, think of how your everyday experience of life is compared with your imagination of yourself as part of the entire Universe. When you normally get up in the morning, your thoughts are probably on mundane tasks, such as preparing breakfast and getting to work. How would your day begin if you remembered where you were on planet Earth, and where Earth is in relation to other planets and to the galaxy in which Earth resides?

3 As you colour, keep the vastness of space in mind. How does this change your view of your life, your problems and your priorities? Do you feel small and insignificant, or part of something much more vast and mysterious? Do you feel the Universe and yourself to be an expression of a Divine intelligence?

4 When you finish colouring your mandala, meditate on any realizations you may have had about yourself as a result of contemplating these questions.

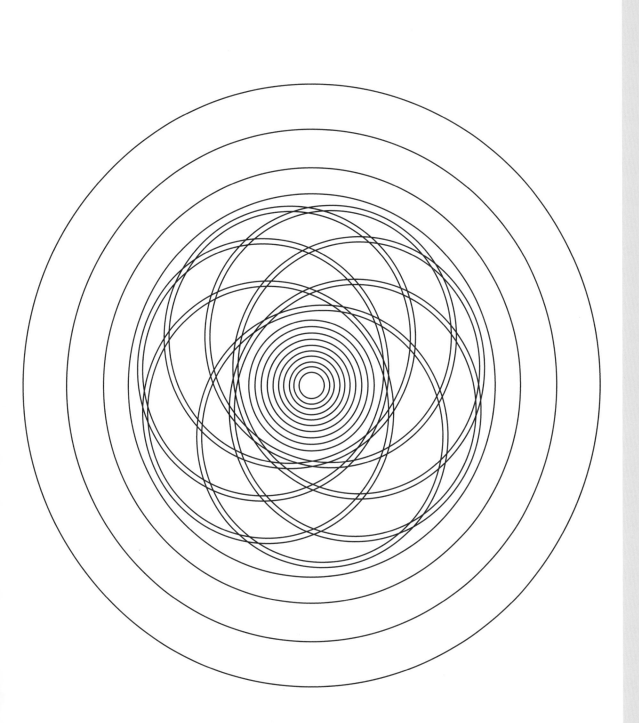

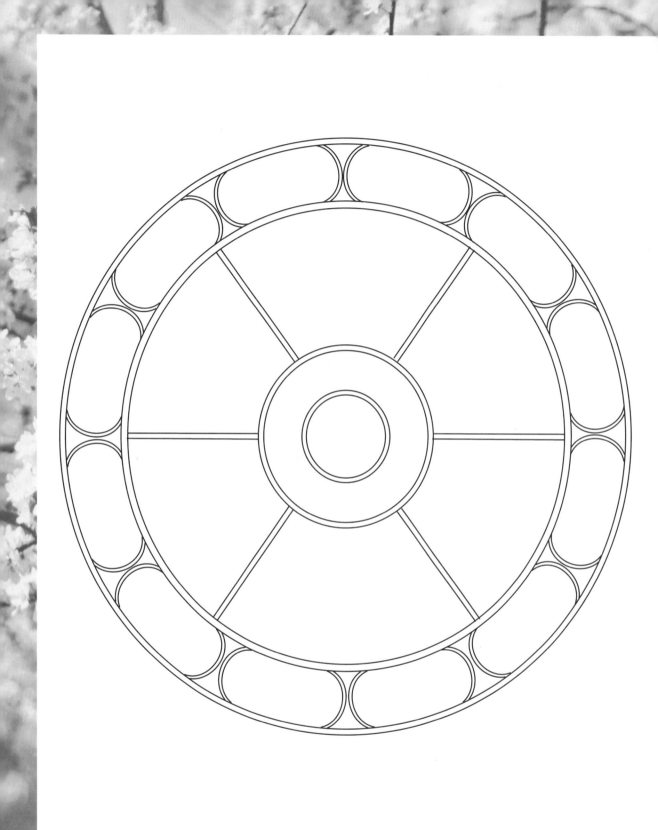

MEDITATION
ON TIME

1 Begin by meditating on your breath for five minutes (see page 24). Try not to think of anything and stay focused on your out-breath. After five minutes note how the passage of time felt for you. Did it pass quickly or did it seem longer than five minutes?

2 Begin colouring the mandala anywhere you desire. As you colour, think about your relationship to time. Do you feel you never have enough time or that there is always time to achieve the things you need to do? Do you procrastinate or use the pressure of time to motivate you to get things done?

3 Think of activities that make time stand still for you or that suspend your sense of the passage of time. Do you forget time when you are reading an exciting novel or watching a film that completely engrosses you? Do you forget what time it is when you are with someone you love?

4 Our sense of time can expand or contract, yet our time on Earth is finite and limited. Think of how you use your time. Are you usually conscious of what you are doing? Do you make good choices for the way you spend your time?

5 If you knew you were going to die in a year, what would you do differently? How would you spend the time you have left? What would you do that you haven't done? What would you stop doing?

6 Complete your mandala and meditate on how you use the precious time you have on Earth.

LABYRINTHS AND MEDITATION

—

A labyrinth is a circular form made up of a single circuitous path. It is an ancient symbol that represents journey, discovery and transformation. As a meditative tool, the labyrinth requires your active participation. You can walk the path of a large labyrinth or use your finger to trace a small version on paper, and examples of each type of meditation are given in this chapter. At its deepest level, the labyrinth is both archetype and metaphor for the journey of life and the journey inwards into your deepest self.

WHAT IS A LABYRINTH?

Labyrinths are sacred geometric forms and structures that have been around for at least 4,000 years. Ancient examples are found in many cultures around the world, including Europe, India and the American states of New Mexico and Arizona. The path created by the labyrinth was designed to be walked, traced or danced as a vehicle for reflection, meditation and prayer.

The first known labyrinth appeared in Crete around 3000 BCE. The exact meaning of the original labyrinth is unknown, but researchers speculate that it was the graphic outline of an ancient Greek dance, in which a line of dancers followed a serpentine path to the centre, perhaps to induce an altered state of consciousness. The first labyrinth image may have been the path of the dance traced on the ground for the dancers to follow.

As a symbol of a spiritual journey and transformation, the labyrinth spread separately from the dance of its origin. For example, during the time of the Crusades, labyrinths symbolized the spiritual pilgrimage to the Holy Land. For the Native American Hopi people, the labyrinth symbolizes death and rebirth and a return to Mother Earth.

THE LABYRINTH'S BASIC STRUCTURE

Alabyrinth is different from a maze. A maze requires you to negotiate its many wrong turns and dead-ends in order to reach its centre. In contrast, a labyrinth has only one continuous path to the centre; you leave by retracing that same path to your starting point. Also, a labyrinth is not a spiral; a labyrinth has a perimeter, whereas a spiral does not.

To better understand the labyrinth's structure it is best to imagine viewing it from above, as if looking down on the foundations of a building from the air (see page 101 for a classical example).

The labyrinth's outside perimeter has only one opening, where the path to the centre begins. The lines themselves create the 'walls' of the labyrinth, and the space between the lines forms the 'path'. The path fills the entire interior space, which is made up of circuits that fold back on themselves, change direction and bring you close to, and then away from, the centre. Each time you enter a different circuit, you turn 180 degrees. As you change direction, you shift your awareness from right brain to left brain, which induces more receptive states of consciousness. Eventually you reach the centre – a place for meditation, prayer or reflection. What you discover or receive there is absorbed and integrated on your walk out.

A METAPHOR FOR SPIRITUAL TRANSFORMATION

The labyrinth form is a beautiful metaphor for spiritual and personal transformation. The surrounding wall and entrance mark the start of a journey, one that takes you away from your normal everyday life and leads you inwards. Inside the labyrinth, the space is very complicated and somewhat confusing. A spiritual journey – one that asks larger questions, such as the purpose of existence, the nature of God or divinity or the reality of good and evil – is not an easy one. It is often filled with doubt; it can be complicated and confusing, and even beginning the journey takes courage and maturity.

The path inside the labyrinth has a maximum number of twists and turns that the space can accommodate, and provides the longest route to the centre. Just as you seem to be reaching the centre, the path takes you away from it. Like the spiritual path, the labyrinthine path is sometimes frustrating and difficult. You may feel it is not worth it, or perhaps that you are not worthy or capable. But if you can stand the anxiety and stress, and don't give up, you will eventually reach the centre.

Once in the centre, you are alone with yourself and God, your higher power – or whatever or whomever you are looking for. This encounter profoundly changes you, and you understand that you can't go back to how and what you were. You make a 180-degree turn and begin following the path back to the entrance, to a new beginning, with new

spiritual realizations to carry you forward. You are not the same person who entered the labyrinth.

Each person's walk is a unique experience. How you walk and what you experience differs with each individual. Some people use the walk for clearing the mind and centring themselves. Others enter with a question or concern. Your time in the centre can be used for receiving, reflecting, meditating or praying, as well as for discovering your own sacred inner space. The walk out provides time for integrating what you have received. Your walk can be a healing or very profound experience, or it can simply be an interesting walk. Whether you are physically walking a labyrinth or tracing one with your finger, each time is unique. There is also a cumulative effect of working with labyrinths over time.

CREATING A LABYRINTH FOR MEDITATION

Interest in the healing and spiritual power of the labyrinth has increased in recent decades, and thousands of new labyrinths have been created around the world. You can locate a labyrinth to walk near you by consulting the labyrinth locater at www.labyrinthsociety. org. There are also hand-held labyrinths that you can purchase, with the path incised into a wood or plastic surface that you can trace with your finger.

For the following meditations you can find a labyrinth to walk, buy a hand-held one or create one yourself. A small labyrinth can either be drawn or painted on a piece of paper, then traced with your finger; or you can draw or paint one on a big piece of canvas for use in a large indoor space. Large labyrinths can be created using masking tape on a school gym floor. You can also create an outdoor labyrinth using stones, bricks, candles, plants or flowers, strings of Christmas-tree lights or anything else you like or

have to hand to mark a path, either temporarily or permanently. If you have access to a beach, you can create a large labyrinth by tracing its path in the sand.

The following diagrams show you how to create a classical seven-circuit labyrinth from Crete. The easiest way is to start with a cross. Then add right angles between the arms of the cross. Place a dot in each right angle. Then connect them in the order shown. If you add an additional right angle, you will get a larger, 11-circuit labyrinth.

LABYRINTH MEDITATIONS

The following meditations are either for a large labyrinth that you walk or for a small labyrinth that you trace with your finger. The meditations are interchangeable and can be adapted for either kind of labyrinth, although suggestions are given below on how they work best.

MEDITATION ON OPENING TO THE LABYRINTH

1 Create or buy a small labyrinth made of paper, wood or any other material that will enable you to trace the path with your finger.

2 Find a time and place to be alone. Breathe deeply for a few minutes with your eyes closed, to relax and focus you. Set the intention that you are going to allow your relationship with your labyrinth to open and deepen.

3 Begin tracing the path with the index finger of your non-dominant hand (the one you do not write with). Move slowly and overcome any desire to race to the centre. Ask the labyrinth for images to help you connect deeply with it. Stop for a moment just before reaching the centre.

4 Lift your finger from the path and place the palm of your non-dominant hand over the centre. As you breathe in, visualize light and energy flowing out of the centre into your hand, arm and up to your heart. As you breathe out, feel the light and energy flowing back, from your heart, down your arm, into your hand and then into the labyrinth's centre.

5 Continue to breathe with the labyrinth and notice any other images that come to mind. When you are ready, end your meditation in the centre, lift your palm and return the index finger of your non-dominant hand to the path.

6 Retrace the path to the entrance, letting yourself absorb the experience.

MEDITATION ON SOLVING A PROBLEM

1 Find or create a labyrinth to walk. Sit or stand at the entrance and contemplate a problem that you need help in solving. It might have to do with money or relationships, work or any other unresolved trouble, large or small. Bring it fully to mind, including any feelings about it that you may have.

2 Create the intention to receive whatever advice or solution your labyrinth walk reveals. Open your heart to whatever the labyrinth has to provide. Be willing to face any truths about yourself or about the situation that may be difficult or challenging to accept.

3 Breathe deeply for a few minutes to clear your mind of any distractions and begin your walk. As you walk, continue to hold the problem – and your intention – in your heart and mind.

4 As you follow the circuit and move closer to and further away from the centre, ask your higher power for help and guidance. Your higher power may be a divinity or simply a manifestation of your own wise self.

5 When you reach the centre, stand or sit there. Again breathe deeply and open yourself to any insights that may illuminate your problem.

6 When you are ready, retrace your steps. Accept whatever you did or did not learn. Write about your walk and your problem. Note any new thoughts, feelings or insights that arise.

MEDITATION ON HEALING ILLNESS

1 Sit or stand at the entrance of the labyrinth. Create the intention that this walk will help to heal you from physical illness or a chronic condition.

2 Begin slowly walking the path and imagine that your immune system is being energized with each step. Create an image of your immune system, such as a pure white light illuminating dark, stagnant areas of your body. Hold that image in your mind as you walk.

3 As you make each turn, alternating from left to right, imagine your body coming into balance, while the purifying and healing white light continues to flood your body.

4 If you are feeling ill as you begin your walk, do not feel discouraged if you do not experience immediate relief. Continue the visualization, knowing that you are asking the Universe to give you the strength and resources to heal eventually. Open your heart to that possibility, even if you are full of doubt and fear.

5 When you finally reach the centre, sit or lie down, if possible. Breathe deeply. Meditate using the visualization of white light filling your body and restoring your health. Remain in the centre for as long as you can maintain the visualization. When you are ready, stand and hold your hands over your heart and accept any healing that you have received.

6 Turn and slowly retrace your steps.

WALKING WITH A SPIRITUAL GUIDE

1 Choose a person or a Divine being who inspires you or for whom you have reverence, to accompany you in your imagination on your labyrinth walk. For example, you might choose Gandhi, God, Jesus, the Virgin Mary, Buddha, Kwan Yin, Martin Luther King, Mother Teresa or Athena.

2 Ask yourself why you have chosen this person or Divine being, and what you would like to discuss.

3 Stand at the entrance of the labyrinth that you are going to walk and imagine the person or being standing beside you.

4 Begin walking the path and simply notice how it feels to walk with such an amazing entity. What emotions come up? Do you feel supported, unworthy, happy or sad?

5 When you reach the centre, sit or stand with your guide and ask him or her a question. It could be a practical one, such as 'Should I start a new career?' Or it could be a more spiritual one, such as 'What is the purpose of living?'

6 Listen to what your guide has to say to you. If there is no answer, simply bask in the joy of being with such a powerful and supportive being.

7 When you are ready, retrace your steps to the entrance with your guide and thank him or her for accompanying you today.

MEDITATION ON FACING FEAR

1 Bring to mind a fear that has been interfering with your life. It could be a specific fear, such as the fear of heights or flying, or a more generalized fear of being a failure or a fear of intimacy.

2 Stand at the entrance of the labyrinth and generate the intention to face your fear at the centre of the labyrinth. Bring your fear to mind and feel it as intensely as you can. Now imagine the fear as three-dimensional. What form does it take? Is it a frightening animal, a monster, an amorphous blob?

3 Now begin your walk with the determination to meet your fear at the centre of the labyrinth. As you walk, let any emotions or thoughts arise. You may feel short of breath, dizzy or want to stop. No matter what you feel, keep going.

4 When you reach the centre, visualize your fear standing there in front of you. Don't worry, your fear will not attack you; it will simply stand there.

5 Face your fear and tell yourself that you will no longer let it interfere with your life. Tell it that it is not going to keep you from enjoying yourself or taking on new challenges. Say anything else you wish, then end your conversation.

6 Turn your back on your fear and retrace your steps.

BREATH MEDITATION TO REDUCE ANXIETY

1 Close your eyes and breathe deeply for a few moments. Give yourself permission to take this time to enable you to meditate and walk your labyrinth.

2 Open your eyes and position yourself or the finger of your non-dominant hand, at the entrance of the labyrinth. Breathe naturally and begin to focus on your breath. When thoughts or worries intervene, simply return to your breath.

3 Begin walking or tracing the path as you continue to focus on your breath.

4 You will notice your attention moving from the path to your breath and back again. Try to maintain your focus on both simultaneously. If anxiety returns, simply let it move on like a cloud in the sky and return to concentrating on the path and your breath.

5 When you reach the centre, if it is a large labyrinth, sit and meditate on your breath for a few minutes. If you are tracing a small labyrinth, place the palm of your non-dominant hand on the centre and meditate on your breath.

6 When you are ready, continue to maintain your focus on your breath and begin the journey back to the entrance. Take your time and do not rush.

7 When you reach the entrance, take a moment to compare how you feel now with the way you felt before you started your labyrinth meditation.

MEDITATION ON ENDING A RELATIONSHIP

1 Find a time and place where you can be alone and undisturbed, then place your small labyrinth on a table in front of you.

2 Bring to mind the person with whom you are ending your relationship. If you are angry, sad or afraid, allow those feelings to emerge.

3 Create the intention that this labyrinth meditation will help you end this relationship in a healthy way.

4 Begin tracing the path with the index finger of your non-dominant hand. Take your time. While you are tracing it, visualize that you are moving towards the centre of your own being – a place of wisdom and strength.

5 When you have completed the path to the centre, place the palm of your non-dominant hand over the centre. Close your eyes and imagine that you are facing the person you are leaving. Thank them for the time you have spent together and wish them well. Now imagine turning and walking away from them.

6 Open your eyes and let any feelings emerge. If you want to cry or laugh, do so. You may feel afraid or very sad. Or you may feel relieved, as if you have just been released from prison. Any and all feelings are acceptable. If you are still clinging to the relationship after having said goodbye, let that be.

7 Begin your journey back out of the labyrinth. Let yourself absorb the experience as you trace it.

MEDITATION ON BALANCING RIGHT AND LEFT BRAIN

1 Stand balanced on both feet, with your spine straight and shoulders relaxed, at the entrance to the labyrinth. Close your eyes and breathe for a few minutes to calm and centre yourself. Remember that your right brain is visual and processes information in an intuitive and simultaneous way, and your left brain is verbal and processes information in an analytical and sequential way.

2 Open your eyes and begin your journey into the labyrinth. On this walk, try not to think of anything. When thoughts or feelings emerge, simply bring your attention to the path. Keep your head facing forwards.

3 When you come to a 180-degree turn, consciously move your head and eyes in the direction that you are heading, keeping them on the path in front. When you come to the next turn, move your body, head and eyes in the new direction. Walk slowly and steadily, with your focus on the path and on your eye movement.

4 When you reach the centre, stand still with your eyes closed. Meditate on your breath for as long as you like. Again, if thoughts or feelings intrude, do not entertain them. When you are ready, open your eyes and begin your journey back in the same way, slowly and carefully, paying attention to the path and to your eye movement.

5 When you reach the entrance, stand for a minute and notice whether you feel any different from when you started.

MEDITATION ON A COMMITTED RELATIONSHIP

1 Stand together with your partner at the entrance of the labyrinth. Close your eyes and breathe deeply for a minute to clear your mind of any expectations or distractions. Open your mind and heart to your partner and bring to mind your commitment to him or her. Mentally dedicate this walk to strengthening your commitment and deepening your relationship.

2 Open your eyes and begin walking the labyrinth, one behind the other. If you wish, you can switch places as you go, trading off taking the lead. Walk slowly and deliberately.

3 As you walk, think about what loving unconditionally means to you. Imagine allowing your partner the freedom to be themselves. Genuinely wish them freedom and happiness.

4 As you continue towards the centre, think about what compromise means to you. How will you empower yourself in this relationship, yet also relinquish control? Commit yourself to finding a balance that allows both of you what you need.

5 When you reach the centre, stand together facing each other. Silently look into each other's eyes for a few minutes. Let whatever thoughts or feelings that emerge flow through you.

6 When you are both ready, begin your journey back to the entrance. How did your experience in the centre affect you?

MEDITATION ON OPENING UP TO CREATIVITY

1 Draw or paint a small labyrinth for use in this meditation, following the instructions on page 101. When you have completed the labyrinth, trace the lines with liquid glue. Before the glue dries, cover the labyrinth with gold or silver glitter. Remove any excess.

2 Place your labyrinth on a table in front of you. Close your eyes, then breathe deeply to clear your mind and prepare to enter the labyrinth.

3 Open your eyes and using the index finger of your non-dominant hand begin to trace the path slowly and deliberately towards the centre. If you have fear about 'letting go' in the creative process, or doubts about your talents or skills, see those hindrances and inhibitions falling away.

4 With each turn, feel yourself getting closer to your creative centre, where you can be uninhibited, joyful, spontaneous and playful. Your creative centre may also be the source of profound spiritual realizations.

5 When you reach the centre, place the palm of your non-dominant hand over it. Put your other palm over your heart. Close your eyes and let the energy flow between your heart and the centre of the labyrinth.

6 When you are ready, open your eyes and begin tracing the path from the centre back to the entrance. As you trace, meditate on the thought that you are a channel for the expression of the profound joy and perennial truths of the Universe.

MEDITATION ON
THE GREAT MOTHER

1 Stand before the entrance of the labyrinth and breathe deeply to calm your mind. Prepare yourself to be embraced by the feminine energies of the labyrinth.

2 As you begin your journey to the centre of the labyrinth, imagine that you are entering the Universe of the Great Mother. You can envision her as the Great Goddess, Mother Earth, the Virgin Mary, the feminine Buddha Tara, the Chinese female bodhisattva Kwan Yin, or any other feminine manifestation of Divine energy that you choose.

3 Walk very slowly and deliberately, and let yourself relax progressively with each step. Imagine that you are being held safely by this emanation of the Divine Feminine. If you feel like crying, let yourself do so.

4 When you reach the centre, stand or sit and close your eyes. Imagine yourself in her presence. Imagine her smiling as she looks lovingly into your eyes. Realize that she is the embodiment of love and compassion. Know that she completely accepts and loves you as you are. Feel her powerful protection and support.

5 When you are ready, open your eyes, thank her and begin your walk back to the entrance. Know that she will be there with you whenever you need to call on her.

MEDITATION TO
FACE THE TRUTH

1 Stand at the entrance of the labyrinth and bring to mind the situation that you want to resolve. Breathe deeply for a few moments and let any feelings about it arise.

2 Begin walking the path to the centre and as you walk imagine that with every step the truth of the situation becomes clearer to you. If you begin to feel fear, know that the protective and supportive energies of the labyrinth will enable you to face whatever you need to face.

3 When you reach the centre, stand and open your heart and mind to whatever you need to know to resolve the situation. You may have a sudden realization about what is necessary or you may still feel confused. What you have done is set in motion the process of solving the problem by opening yourself to the truth, which you may have wished to avoid.

4 When you are ready, begin your walk back to the entrance. Let yourself experience any feelings or ponder any thoughts that may have emerged.

NATURE AND MEDITATION

—

Nature soothes, nature heals. Beauty and wisdom await you in a fragrant pine wood, on a deserted beach, by a still pond or a flowing stream. If you don't have time to get out into the wild in order to meditate, then simply meditating in the nearest park or in your own back garden will do. Try one of the meditations on the following pages to reconnect yourself to the beauties of nature and to the truths that nature holds.

THE NEED TO RECONNECT WITH NATURE

Many of us who live in cities and spend most of our lives indoors have lost our connection to the natural world. This disconnection – with trees, wild flowers, the fox and the wren – has had consequences for our environment and for our souls. We have become dysfunctional in many ways and separation from nature has certainly contributed to our global problems.

The following are simple meditations to help you reconnect, both for your own benefit and for the planet we call home. There is no need to record them – simply read the appropriate meditation, put the book down and meditate. Eventually you can develop your own meditations that resonate with your unique experience of the natural world.

MEDITATION ON CLOUDS

1 Pick a day when the sky is blue and the clouds are white and plentiful. Find a place outdoors where you can see the clouds in the sky. If you like, lie down on the grass for a better view.

2 Take in the feeling of looking up into the vastness above. If you are like most people, you may actually forget to look up at the sky for days or weeks on end. You know it's there, but your eyes are mostly focused (indoors or out) straight ahead.

3 Breathe deeply for a moment and note to yourself how this feels. What thoughts come to mind?

4 Notice how the clouds move and change. Whether moving fast or slowly, they are in constant flux. They do not stay the same from one second to the next. Realize that you are like the clouds. You too are not the same from one moment to the next. Nothing is fixed or static, in you or in nature.

5 Contemplate this idea and let your thoughts and emotions emerge and disappear like the clouds above you. Why cling to them?

MEDITATION ON BIRDS

1 Get yourself to a park or if you have the time, go out into the country. Find a place where you can be alone and where you can hear and see birds. A small wood or a large hedge often serves as shelter for many birds.

2 Stand or sit down on the ground, if possible. Breathe deeply to settle yourself. Close your eyes and listen. How many different bird calls do you hear?

3 Try not to think of anything. Maintain your slow, deep breathing and just take in the sounds. Let their various songs fill your mind and heart. Stay with this conscious listening for as long as you like.

4 How did it change you? Do you feel calmer or uplifted? Do you feel sad or emotional in any way?

5 Now open your eyes and try to see the birds in the branches above. Notice how they move, dance and fly. Notice their speed and energy, the colour and beauty of their feathers and their fragility. Generate a feeling of gratitude for their existence and their ever-present companionship.

MEDITATION ON WATER

1 Find a secluded spot near a natural body of water. It could be a small pond, a stream, a river, a lake or an ocean. It can be large or small, moving or still.

2 Stand or sit as close as you can to the water's edge. Notice the water's quality. Is it still and peaceful or full of movement? Is it fresh or salty, clear or muddied? What colour or colours is it? Does it sparkle or is it dull? How does it smell?

3 At this time, imagine all the water on the Earth being protected and well cared for. Imagine the streams, lakes and rivers being cleared of all pollution. Visualize the underground aquifers as safe and healthy. See the oceans clean and teeming with fish, and the large sea mammals happy in their environment. Given the decline in the health of our waters, this may sound impossible, but imagination represents the beginning of change. Meditating on a clean, protected and cherished water supply adds energy towards this happening.

MEDITATION ON THE NIGHT SKY

1 Pick a clear, starry night and a place where you can be alone. If necessary, go to a place where there are few city lights to obstruct your view. Sit or lie down on a blanket and look up at the night sky.

2 Feel yourself fall into the blackness above you, and marvel at the stars and planets that sparkle like diamonds.

3 How does looking up at the incomprehensible vastness of the Universe make you feel? Does it put your worries into perspective? Feel a sense of interconnectedness with all space and time, with everyone who has lived and will live. Imagine the Buddha, Jesus, Moses or your own chosen Divine being staring up at the stars – the same ones you are looking at now.

4 Stay as long as it feels right. Try to still your mind and let the experience envelop you. When you get home, write down any thoughts, realizations or feelings that emerged.

MEDITATION IN A PINE FOREST

1 From ancient times, humans have considered pines the most sacred of trees. Deciduous trees shed their leaves, yet pines remain green, suggesting an eternal nature. Initially, pines were worshipped for themselves, and later they were considered to form the sacred abodes of gods and spirits. Even today some Mongolian tribes will ride silently through a pine forest so as not to disturb the resident spirits. Whether you believe they contain spirits or not, pine forests are wonderful places for meditation.

2 Locate a pine forest or a stand of pines where you can be alone and undisturbed. Bring a blanket and sit on the pine-needled floor.

3 Breathe in the pine scent and let it clear your heart and mind of any worry or fear. Feel the energy of the pines surrounding and protecting you. Notice the quiet and the soft sound of the wind in the boughs.

4 Meditate on the nourishing aspect of Mother Earth, and on the sacredness of all creation.

MEDITATION ON
THE SEASONS

1 There are four days in the year that are perfect for meditating on the meaning of the seasons. They are the spring equinox, the summer solstice, the autumn equinox and the winter solstice. Find a calendar that notes them or check on the Internet for the dates.

2 On the solstice or equinox that you are celebrating, find an appropriate place to meditate that feels right to you. It can be indoors or outdoors. You may choose to stand, sit or walk. Create a form of meditation that makes sense to you.

3 After choosing how and where you are going to meditate, use the seasonal change to meditate on the topic of change and impermanence. How do you handle change, and do you accept that all things are impermanent and will end? Notice that change and endings can be both sad and devastating and happy and liberating. How you respond to life has a lot to do with how you experience it. Allowing yourself to meditate on the reality of impermanence will help you handle and accept change with grace.

MEDITATION
ON FLOWERS

1 Flowers offer one of the most stunning displays of nature, and the best way to enjoy them is outdoors in a garden setting. It is here – in the company of insects, the sun, the rain and the earth – that you can best experience the overwhelming, and sometimes breathtaking, beauty of nature.

2 If possible, meditate on flowers in your own back garden; alternatively, go to a park or a botanical garden.

3 Sit or stand in front of flowers that attract you. Close your eyes, breathe deeply and take in their perfume. Open your eyes and let their form and colour flood your vision. Notice any insects buzzing around them – perhaps a bee or a butterfly. Try not to think about the flowers; just let them enter and permeate your consciousness. Are you smiling?

MEDITATION
ON FIRE

1 Meditation on an external object builds focus and concentration. One of the best objects for meditation is fire or a flame. It can be a candle, a fire in your fireplace or an outdoor bonfire. As humans we naturally gravitate towards fire and have a fascination for it – perhaps because it is primal and essential for our existence. In nature, the fire element heats, burns and transforms.

2 Seat yourself near a candle flame or fire, either on a cushion in traditional meditation posture or on a chair with your feet flat on the ground and your spine straight. Close your eyes and take three deep breaths. Now open your eyes and focus on the flame or fire. Try not to let thoughts or emotions intrude. When they do, simply return to gazing single-mindedly at the flame or fire.

3 Meditate in this way for a minimum of ten minutes. If possible, do this on a daily basis for one month and notice how it affects your ability to focus and concentrate in your everyday life.

GLOSSARY

Allah: The Arabic word for 'God' used by Muslims to refer to God. In Islam, Allah is considered the only deity, the creator of the Universe, and the ultimate judge of humankind. Muslim scholars consider Allah to be the same as Yahweh who made a covenant with Abraham and the Jews, however, the sacred book of the Muslim faith, the Qur'an, portrays Allah as both more powerful and more remote than Yahweh. Allah is understood as a universal deity, whereas, Yahweh was considered more closely associated with the Israelites. According to the Islamic tradition, there are more than 99 Names of God each evoking a distinct aspect of Allah. The most famous and most frequent of these names are 'the Merciful' (*al-rahman*) and 'the Compassionate' (*al-rahim*).

Atman: is a philosophical term used within Hinduism to identify the soul. It is one's true self that is not identified with worldly existence. Some schools of Hinduism see the soul within each living person as being identical with Brahman, or the all-pervading soul of the Universe. Other schools differentiate between the individual *atman* in living beings, and the Supreme, all-pervading *atman* considering them as being at least partially separate. Thus *atman* can be used to describe an individual soul or Braham, the soul of the Universe, depending on the speaker's philosophical point of view.

Buddha: Buddha is a Sanskrit word meaning awakened. In Buddhism, a buddha is any being who has become fully awakened or enlightened, and has experienced Nirvana.

Buddhists do not consider the historical Siddhartha Gautama to have been the only Buddha. The Hinayana or older tradition of Buddhism refers to 28 previous Buddhas, while the later Mahayana tradition also mentions many Buddhas who are celestial in nature such as Amitabha or Vairocana. All Buddhists across the spectrum believe that the next Buddha will be one named Maitreya. All Buddhist traditions hold that a Buddha has completely purified his or her mind of desire, aversion and ignorance and thus become fully awakened. He or she has realized the ultimate truth, the non-dualistic nature of life, and thus ended, for him or herself, the suffering that those who have not awakened experience in life.

In Mahayana Buddhism, the Buddha is thought to be no longer an ordinary human being, but rather has entered the ultimate transcendental 'body/mind' known as Dharmakaya. He or she is considered to have eternal and infinite life, to be present in all things referred to as the boundless *dharmadhatu*, and possessed of great and immeasurable qualities beyond comprehension.

A common misconception among Westerners is that the Buddha is the Buddhist counterpart to God. Buddhism, however, is non-theistic. It does not teach the existence of a supreme creator god or depend on any supreme being for enlightenment. Rather, the Buddha is a guide and teacher who points the way for others to becoming fully awakened, and to becoming a Buddha themselves.

Devi: The word Devi is the Sanskrit word for 'Goddess.' As The Great Goddess of the Hindu religion, she has many identities. She is at times depicted as gentle and approachable and at other times as ferocious and wrathful. In her guise as Mother of the Universe, she reigns over the cosmos, destroying evil and creating and destroying entire worlds. She is worshipped using many names often reflecting local customs and ritual, and throughout India she is celebrated in song and poem. For some she is their primary deity while for others she is part of a greater pantheon including Shiva, Vishnu, Ganesha and Surya. All Hindu goddesses may be viewed as different manifestations of Devi.

Dharana: A sanskrit term meaning concentration or single focus; *Dharana* is the sixth limb of Patanjali's Eight Limbs of Yoga. *Dharana* is the initial step of deep concentrative meditation, where the object being focused upon is held in the mind without consciousness wavering from it. In this step, the object of meditation, the meditator, and the act of meditation itself remain separate. That is, the meditator or the meditator's higher awareness is conscious of meditating on an object, and of his or her own self, which is concentrating on the object.

Dhyana: A sanskrit word for a type or aspect of meditation that focuses on concentration and mental stability. It is the seventh limb of Patanjali's Eight Limbs of Yoga and a key concept in both Hinduism, and Buddhism. In *Dhyana*, as the meditator becomes more advanced consciousness of the act of meditation disappears, and only the consciousness of being/existing and the object of concentration exist in the mind.

Higher Power: A personal understanding of an external power greater than one's self, often considered to be Jesus, God, Buddha, Mary, Allah or other divine figure, Alternately, 'higher power' may refer to your higher self or your own innate wisdom.

Kabbalah: The Hebrew word 'Kaballah' means to receive and refers to the communication between God and Moses. Kabbalah is mystical form of the Jewish religion that places emphasis on the symbolism of syllables and numbers.

Meridians: Energy channels in the body that circulate 'chi' or life energy. Chinese acupuncturists use the 2000 recognized points along the twelve major meridians to insert needles to treat various illnesses and balance *chi* energy.

Natural Stress Relief: Natural Stress Relief is a non-religious mantra meditation technique, practised for the purpose of reducing stress, anxiety, nervousness, mild depression, insomnia, phobias, and for improvement of wellbeing.

Niyama: Niyama is a Sanskrit word meaning 'rules' or 'laws.' This is the second Limb of Pantanjali's Eight Limbs of Yoga. *Niyama* are the rules prescribed for personal observance and refer to the attitude we adopt toward ourselves. There are five *Niyama* in Pananjali's system. The first *Niyama* is *Saucha*, or cleanliness and has both an inner and an outer aspect. Outer cleanliness means keeping ourselves clean. Inner cleanliness has to do with maintaining the health of our bodily organs and clarity of mind. The second is *Santosa* and is the feeling of being content or happy with what we have. Literally the word means happiness. The real meaning of *Santosa* is to accept whatever happens in life. The third, *Tapas*, refers to the sustained practice of keeping the body fit through paying attention to what we eat, attention to body posture, attention to breathing patterns in order to keep the body fit and functioning well. The fourth *Niyama* is *Svadhyaya*.
It means to get close to oneself, that is, to study oneself in order to reduce unwanted and destructive tendencies. *Isvara Pranidhara* means to contemplate on God in order to become attuned to god and god's will.

Paratyahara: The fifth element among the Eight Limbs of Patanjali's Yoga, in which the consciousness of the individual is internalized in order that the sensations from the senses of taste, touch, sight, hearing and smell don't reach their respective receptors in the brain. This is sometimes accomplished by concentrating on the third eye, or the point between the eyebrows. With this, the person meditating is free to meditate without distractions. At advanced stages breath control is used to still the electrical currents that pulsate through the nervous system.

Pranayama: *Pranayama* is the fourth 'limb' of the Eight Limbs of Patanjali's Yoga and relates to the control of the breath that is accomplished through the practice of various breathing techniques. One technique is called 'Ujjayi' or the 'sounding' breath or 'ocean sounding' breath. It involves constricting the back of the throat while breathing to create an 'ah' sound. Another is 'Dirgha' known as the 'complete' or 'three-part' breath. This breathing technique teaches how to fill the three chambers of the lungs, beginning with the lower lungs. Several researchers have reported that *Pranayama* techniques are beneficial in treating a range of stress related disorders. Practitioners report that the practice of *Pranayama* develops a steady mind, strong will-power, and sound judgement, extends life and enhances perception.

Salat: A ritual prayer practised by Muslims five times each day in supplication to Allah. *Salat* is compulsory for all adult Muslims and is considered the most important act of worship in Islam.

Samadhi: Hindu and Buddhist term that describes a meditative state of consciousness in which the meditator becomes one with the object of meditation and in which the mind becomes completely still, and devoid of all thought. It is considered a precursor for enlightenment in Buddhism, and is the eighth and final limb of Pantanjali's Eight Limbs of Yoga.

Shiva: One of the principal deities of Hinduism viewed as the supreme deity. In some branches of Hinduism he is worshipped as one of the five manifestations of the divine, the other four being Vishnu, Devi, Ganesha, and Surya. Followers of Hinduism who focus their worship upon Shiva are called *Shaivites*. Another approach to the divinities in Hinduism identifies Brahma, Vishnu, and Shiva as each representing one of the three primary aspects of the divine in Hinduism. In this system Brahma is the creator, Vishnu is the maintainer or preserver, and Shiva is the destroyer or transformer.

Yama: The first of Pantanjali's Eight Limbs of Yoga, the word yama is sanskrit for 'restraint.' There are five eithical guidelines, or 'yamas' regarding moral behavior towards others. These are often called the 'don'ts' of Yogic philosophy. One way to approach the *Yamas* is to turn them into something positive. For example, the first, *Ashima*, says to avoid all forms of violence to self and others. One way to work with *Ashima* is to practise love and compassion for all sentient beings. The second, *Satya*, is about refraining from deception and dishonesty. Better to focus on truthfulness with self and others. The third, *Brahmacharya*, asks the practitioner to avoid lust but a better approach is to practice kindness in all sexual relations. *Asteya* means to avoid stealing. A more positive way to practise *Asteya* is to respect and protect what belongs to others. The last, *Aparigraha*, asks the practitioner to avoid greed. A better approach might be to practise generosity.

INDEX

ACKNOWLEDGEMENTS

PICTURE ACKNOWLEDGEMENTS

123RF Branislav Ostojic 8; Julia Sudnitskaya 6l, 29bl; Maksim Pasko 14, 15r, 81c; natbasil 81ar; Rutchapong Moolvai 2, 49ar; serezniy 20; Yulia Grogoryeva 71, 127; **Dreamstime. com** Alexey Poprotskiy 29c, 123; Galyna Andrushko 87ar; Nongnuch Leelaphasuk 29br, 38c, 79; Tomert 86; kickimages 55; sihasakprachum 54; **Octopus Publishing Group** Russell Sadur 35, 36, 39, 40b, 42, 45, 47b, 56-65, 72-74, 76-78; Ruth Jenkinson 23, 24; **Pixabay** 9br, 12r, 49bl, 82br, 120ac; **Shutterstock** JoLin 95; **Unsplash** Adrian González Simón 37l, 81br; Aleksandr Kozlovskii 114, 119al; Ales Krivec 32, 40al, 51, 121ar; Alex Klopcic 19, 22l; Alex Ruban 87cr, 102l; Anna Jimenez Calaf 119ac; Anthony Delanoix 28, 38r; Ashley Batz 26r, 97bl; Ben White 106l; Caroline Grondin 69; Chris Ensey 49al; Clem Onojeghuo 9c, 9ar, 13, 15, 16al, 102c; Colin Maynard 120ar; Colin McMurry 47al; Daniil Kuzelev 26c, 87al; Das Sasha 29al, 38l; Dawid Zawila 102r; Deniz Altindas 107; Denys Nevozhai 67bl, 121ac; Ellen Jantsch 97c; Emma Hall 104l; Erol Ahmed 33, 67ar, 104c; Freestocks 108, 110, 112ar; Gabriel Garcia Marengo 115bl; Gabriel Santiago 115br; Gaetano Cessati 17r, 87bl; Galen Crout 67al, 112ac; Guillaume de Germain 26l; Hans Vivek 85; Harli Marten 88; Harshal Hirve 47ac, 115c; Igor Ovsyannykov 9bl, 11a, 68, 112al; Jay Dantinne 97br; Jez Timms 70, 115al, 120al, Jon Phillips 109; Jose Murillo 66, 67br, 119ar; Josefa Holland Merten 67c; Kari Shea 9al, 12l; Katherine Hanlon 97ar; Keghan Crossland 22c; Kelly Sikkema 21; Larm Rmah 115ar; Laura Esculcas 105; Linda Xu 103; Lukasz Szmigiel 37r; Marcus Dall Col 27; Matt Antonioli 49c, 96; Matthew Kane 2; Melinda Pack 47ar; Melissa Askew 29ar; Michael D Beckwith 80; Mike Enerio 43l, 113; Mr Robot 16ar, 104r; Nick Karvounis 16b, 120b; Olivia Henry 121b; Pamela Nhlengethwa 43c, 81al, 111; Peignault Laurent 97al; Peter Hershey 87cla; Ray Hennessy 22r, 75, 87br; Ren Ran 17l, 25; Ruben Engel 112b; Ryan Hutton 92; Sabine Schulte 6r, 91; Sebastian Unrau 37c, 40ar, 119b; Silvestri Matteo 49br; Stephanie Cotton 7, 81bl; Steven Kamenar 43ar, 121al; Sweet Ice Cream Photography 48; Tim Mossholder 87clb; Timothy Meinberg 6c, 50; Todd Quackenbush 106c, 116; Yoann Boyer 106r.